NOVELTY CLOCKS

FOR WOODWORKERS

NOVELTY CLOCKS

FOR WOODWORKERS

RAYMOND HAIGH

CASSELL

All the line illustrations have
been drawn by the author.

Cassell
Wellington House
125 Strand
London WC2R 0BB

First published 1995
First paperback edition 1996

Distributed in the United States
by Sterling Publishing Co., Inc.
387 Park Avenue South, New York,
NY 10016-8810

Distributed in Australia
by Capricorn Link (Australia) Pty Ltd
2/13 Carrington Road
Castle Hill
NSW 2154

British Library Cataloguing-in-Publication Data
A catalogue record for this book is available from
the British Library

ISBN 0 304 34863 5

Typeset in Method Limited, Epping, Essex
Printed and bound in Slovenia by Printing house DELO – Tiskarna
by arrangement with Korotan – Ljubljana

CONTENTS

INTRODUCTION

I hope that these novelty clocks will captivate and delight the woodworkers who make them and all who use them to measure the passing of the hours. The collection includes whimsical, comical and surreal creations, together with some out-of-the-ordinary timepieces that are just meant to be eye-catching.

Construction and finishing involve an absolute minimum of inexpensive and readily available materials and tools. Full-size patterns are given for all the clocks, and if the detailed, step-by-step guidance is followed patiently, no difficulty should be experienced in making them. Power fretsaw enthusiasts looking for something different will find working on these timepieces particularly enjoyable and rewarding.

Woodworkers who feel reluctant to attempt the kind of colour schemes shown in the photographs should not be discouraged. The clocks are built up in layers from basic shapes, which are painted before assembly, and this eliminates most of the need for skilful brushwork. The three-dimensional effect created by this layering process can be further enhanced by a simple colour-shading technique, and constructors will be surprised how easy it is to improve the appearance of the clocks in this way.

Pendulums swinging; eyes rolling; wings waving; legs and tails wagging; mice hiding; birds, flowers and balloons swaying: these brightly coloured clocks are sure to give pleasure, and maybe even raise an eyebrow or two in surprise.

Moon pendulum

1 MATERIALS, TOOLS AND EQUIPMENT

CONSTRUCTION MATERIALS

Hardboard

Hardboard is used for the construction of all the clocks. Produced from wet fibres compressed at high pressure and temperature, this material is so commonplace it hardly warrants description. The standard variety, ⅛ in (3 mm) thick with one smooth face, is perfectly adequate. However, if constructors are lucky enough to be able to obtain tempered board, its use is to be preferred. Impregnated with resin, this often darker-coloured material is harder and more resistant to fraying when cut into intricate shapes.

Standard hardboard is sold by do-it-yourself and builders' merchants throughout the United Kingdom, Australia, Canada and the USA, and no difficulty should be experienced in obtaining supplies. Resist any temptation to substitute plywood for parts where hardboard is specified, as the colouring and finishing procedures rely on the paper-smooth surface of the latter. It is also wise to stick to the standard ⅛ in (3 mm) thick material, as the use of a thicker board could cause quartz movement spindle-length problems with some of the built-up designs.

Plywood

Plywood is suggested as an alternative to hardboard for the Duck and Ducklings clock dial (page 32) because of the swirling water effect produced when the grain pattern is stained blue.

Plywood is also recommended for the base of the Mad Mouser clock (page 66). Here the natural grain of the wood seems more appropriate around the mouse hole. Use ³⁄₁₆ in (5 mm) thick, pine-faced material for these applications. The variable grain density of pine ensures that pronounced swirling patterns will result from the staining process.

Thinner, ¹⁄₁₆ in (1.5 mm), plywood is used to form the assemblies which connect eyes and tails to the quartz movement pendulum arms. It is also used for dial parts which require a thinner material than the ⅛ in (3 mm) hardboard. The high quality plywood retailed by model shops for building model boats is strongly recommended for this application.

Even thinner, ¹⁄₃₂ in (0.8 mm) or ¹⁄₆₄ in (0.4 mm), plywood is used for eye and eyelid mounts, and for some of the decorative features on the clocks. This material is only retailed by model shops and is fairly expensive to buy in full sheets. Small pieces can usually be purchased, however.

Card is not a very satisfactory substitute for the thin plywood. It cannot be filed and sanded to a finished profile, and it lacks rigidity.

Wood Blocks and Strips

Wall stand-off blocks have to be glued to the backs of some of the dials. These can be cut from scrap lengths of planed softwood.

The base of the Mad Mouser clock (page 66) is trimmed with ¼ × ¼ in (6 × 6 mm) softwood strip. Suitable material can be obtained from do-it-yourself outlets and model shops.

Plastic Wood

Plastic wood is used to form eyelids and Chuckaloo Tutu's beak (page 89). It is also extremely useful for making good any blemishes in the other dial parts. Choose a product comprising wood dust and a cellulose binder. Chalky decorators' fillers are not suitable.

Nuts, Bolts, Screws and Wire

Small nuts, bolts, woodscrews, and self-tapping screws are required for some of the clocks. Many constructors will already have suitable items in their workshops, but if not, model shops are usually able to supply them. In the parts lists which are given for each clock design, these items are specified by their length and approximate diameter, as the type of thread is of no consequence.

Small self-tapping screws are used when screw fixings have to be made to either hardboard or plywood. Driving their parallel threads into pre-drilled holes causes less disturbance and produces a stronger grip than the tapered threads of ordinary wood screws.

Thin wire is required to form pendulum hangers; to attach birds, flowers, stars and balloons to the pendulum assemblies; and to connect up the moving parts of the Mad Mouser clock (page 66). Brass wire is best for this purpose, as it is easy to bend to the required shape, but steel piano wire can be used if desired. Brass and steel wire, together with brass rods, tubes, sheets and strips in a range of interconnecting sizes, are retailed by model shops throughout the United Kingdom, Australia, Canada and the USA.

Constructors who do not live within easy travelling distance of a model shop should contact one or more of the mail-order firms which advertise in magazines devoted to model-making.

Quartz Movements

Junghans quartz-regulated movements power all the clocks in this collection. They are inexpensive, reliable and very typical of the type of movement produced by a number of manufacturers and distributed worldwide.

The basic 738 movement is illustrated in Fig. 1 and the 717 pendulum model in Fig. 2. Early versions of the pendulum movement incorporate

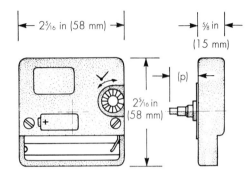

Fig. 1:
Typical quartz movement.
Spindle projection (p) varies: see page 10.

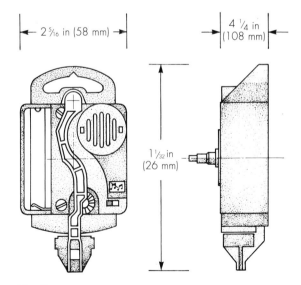

Fig. 2:
Junghans 717 pendulum movement.

the chiming chamber, even when this facility is not included: the chamber is omitted from the latest, non-chiming models. A clip-on wire clock hanger is supplied with the 738. A hanger is formed as part of the case moulding of the 717 pendulum unit.

Most manufacturers supply movements in alternative spindle lengths: short (7/16 in, 11 mm), medium (5/8 in, 16 mm) and long (7/8 in, 21.5 mm). Spindle length is measured from the front of the movement case to the tip of the hand shaft ('p' in Fig. 1). The relevant parts lists indicate which spindle length is required for a particular clock.

Plywood assemblies have to be attached to the plastic pendulum arms of some of the clocks with moving parts. The drawings and guidance given in Chapter 2 assume the use of a Junghans 717 movement. The basic design of the assembly is very simple, and constructors should have no difficulty in adapting it to suit other manufacturers' units. It is important, however, to ensure that the plastic pendulum arm is located at the rear (most of them are) and that the movement case is not too large: if it is, it may not be possible to incorporate the moving eyes in clocks built to the patterns given in this book.

Quartz movements can be obtained from a number of the mail-order suppliers who advertise in craft and woodworking magazines. It is a good idea to ask for a few catalogues before ordering, because several types of movement are available and prices vary significantly.

Hands, Dial Markers and Numerals

Mail-order firms which retail the quartz movements usually also stock a range of hands, dial markers and numerals. The styles of hands depicted in the drawings and colour photographs represent only a small sample of the wide variety currently available.

The size of a pair of hands is the length – pivot to tip – of the minute hand. If a second hand is to be fitted, the movement must be supplied with an open hand-fixing nut. A blind nut is required when there is no second hand. Fig. 9 on page 23 makes the hand-fixing arrangements clear.

Plastic numerals used in cake decoration can be pressed into service. (They mark the dial of Salvador's Watch described on page 112.) Stocked by confectioners' suppliers, they are sometimes available in unusual styles and smaller sizes. Rub-down transfer numerals are considered on page 15.

Adhesives

Balsa cement or a similar, clear, rapid-hardening adhesive is suitable for all of the construction work. Impact (or contact) adhesives are unsatisfactory, and white PVA woodworker glue can only be used for some of the tasks. Cyanoacrylate adhesive (Superglue) produces a strong bond, within seconds, between any combination of the materials used in the construction of the clocks. It is, however, well known for its skin-bonding properties and is relatively expensive!

Whatever adhesive is used, constructors should carefully follow the manufacturer's instructions regarding ventilation and other safety aspects.

Beads, Balls and Cotton Thread

Beads for the Dancing Clown's nose (page 47), Jenny's earrings (page 60), Chuckaloo Tutu's eyes (page 89), and the beans on the Swinging Sausage breakfast plate (page 115), can be bought from shops which sell dressmaking materials or from craft shops. Craft shops also sell wooden balls suitable for Coco's nose (page 42). A reel of cotton thread for binding wires prior to gluing can usually be purloined from the household sewing basket.

The simple tools used for constructing the clocks. The parts for Tom have been cut out and the pattern for Jenny is being transferred to primed hardboard. Note the plastic wood eyelids on the plywood mount and the plastic wood nose.

CONSTRUCTION TOOLS AND EQUIPMENT

The following tools and equipment should be regarded as essential if all the clocks in this book are to be constructed:

1 tracing paper and pencil
2 compasses
3 steel ruler, 12 in (300 mm)
4 fretsaw and blades
5 junior hacksaw
6 Stanley knife or modelling knife and spare blades
7 small hand drill with ⅓₂, ¹⁄₁₆, ³⁄₃₂, ⅛ and ¼ in (0.8, 1.5, 2, 3 and 6 mm) drill bits
8 long-nosed pliers
9 small files: flat, half-round and round
10 medium and fine grade (garnet) abrasive paper
11 small screwdriver

The following additional items will be found useful:

12 fretsaw table
13 dovetail or back saw
14 brace or drill with a ⅜ in (10 mm) bit
15 wire cutters
16 four or more large, sprung paper clips

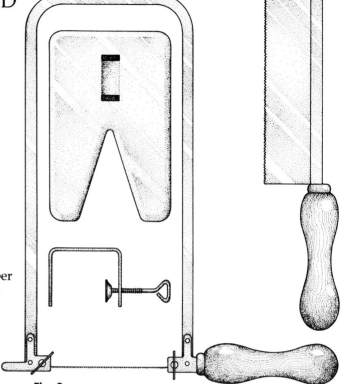

Fig. 3:
Fretsaw, fretsaw table and back saw.

Notes on the above

The tracing paper (1), compasses (2), and steel ruler (3) are used when transferring the patterns to the hardboard. Draughtsman's tracing paper is sold in artists' supply shops, and the compasses should be capable of drawing circles ranging from ³⁄₁₆ in (5 mm) to 4⅝ in (120 mm) radius: a pencil attachment in the compasses described on page 15 would be an ideal arrangement. The steel ruler doubles up as a straight edge for use with the Stanley knife.

The fretsaw (4) is by far the most used item of equipment. No. 6 blades (16 teeth per inch or 25 mm) are satisfactory for both hardboard and plywood, and were used for all the fretsaw work on the clocks. However, more robust No. 9s, (with 13 teeth per inch or 25 mm) will cut hardboard more quickly and may be preferred where the shapes are not too intricate. Similarly, constructors may wish to try a No. 1 blade (25 teeth per inch or 25 mm) when cutting the thin plywood.

The saw cuts on the down stroke, so fit the blades with the teeth pointing towards the handle. Clamp the blade at the handle first, then compress the frame by pressing it against the work bench and clamp the other end of the blade. Pliers may be needed to tighten the wing nuts, and the blade should be taut enough to twang when plucked.

The fretsaw table (12) is clamped to the edge of the work bench. Cutting takes place at the sharp end of the V-shaped notch and better support is given to the material being cut (as well as protection for the edge of the work bench or table).

The dovetail or back saw (13) makes continuous straight cutting easier (e.g. pendulum rods, the plinth parts on the Mad Mouser clock, page 66, and the straight sun rays on the Sun, Moon and Stars clock, page 123). Worked at a shallow angle, it will also reduce large panels of hardboard to more manageable proportions. Fretsaw, fretsaw table, and back saw are illustrated in Fig. 3.

Although useful for light cutting in metal, the junior hacksaw (5) is mainly required for removing the plastic hanger mouldings from the pendulum movements in three of the clocks.

The hand drill (7) is needed for forming entry holes for the fretsaw blades, and holes for bolts, screws and wires. The brace and bit or larger drill (14) is used as an alternative to the fretsaw for forming the quartz-movement spindle holes. Both the ⅜ in (10 mm) bit or drill, and the ¼ in (6 mm) drill mentioned in (7), must be the type equipped with cutters which slice a circle in the wood before the auger begins to remove waste material. This preliminary cutting action prevents the wood or hardboard rupturing around the hole.

Some parts are best cut from thin plywood with a Stanley knife or modelling knife (6). This tool can also be used for the preliminary shaping of eyelids, noses and beaks, but a surgeon's scalpel is better for these tasks.

Long-nosed pliers (8) are used for bending wire parts into shape. Files (9) and abrasive papers (10) smooth the edges of sawn parts before finishing and assembly. The paper clips (16) should be of the large, blue steel variety; they act as inexpensive clamps, holding parts together while the glue is setting.

COLOURING AND FINISHING MATERIALS

White Emulsion Paint

White household emulsion paint is used as a universal primer to produce a suitable surface for the application of the colours. Use the matt rather than the silk or semi-gloss variety, and avoid low-priced economy brands which can contain coarse, chalky pigments. The left-overs from decorating jobs will often yield enough material. If the paint contains gritty particles, strain it through a piece of

nylon. Do not attempt to use oil-based primers. They are not compatible with the colouring process described later.

Poster Paints

Poster paints are used to colour the clocks. Younger readers may still be using them, and those of us who are a little older will certainly remember them from our school days. Sold in small jars, they obliterate well, have a good degree of permanence and can be applied one colour over another. They are inexpensive and, above all, extremely easy and convenient to use.

The colour schemes given for each clock are very arbitrary and can certainly be modified to suit individual tastes. However, if all of the clocks are to be constructed, the following range of colours will probably be required:

poster red or vermilion
mid yellow
ultramarine (a fairly deep blue)
turquoise (a lighter blue sometimes called blue lake)
orange
purple
poster green or mid green
brown
white
black

The above colours mix well to produce a range of shades. Strictly speaking, a palette of red, yellow, blue, white and black would suffice. In practice, however, the pre-mixed orange, green and brown save effort and ensure consistency, and a manufacturer's purple is a far more brilliant colour than can be obtained by combining red and blue.

Varnish

Matt polyurethane clear varnish is used to protect the water-soluble poster colours and produce a washable surface that will withstand a modest amount of handling. It has surprisingly little effect

The equipment used for colouring and finishing the clocks. The ruling pen and the compasses with a pen attachment are optional, but they do make it easy to produce perfect colour boundaries on the rainbow. The upper half of the colour sample board has had three coats of varnish.

on the hue or brilliance of most of the colours. Greens tend to deepen a little, however, while purple becomes brighter and more intense. Use *interior* grade varnish made by a reputable manufacturer. This is less viscous and has greater transparency than exterior varnishes which have to resist the weather.

Wood Dyes

The plywood dial of the Duck and Ducklings clock (page 32) is stained blue to simulate swirling water. Blue wood dyes are sold by specialist craft shops but the expense is hardly justified for such a small quantity. Cobalt blue drawing ink can be used instead. The brilliance of the colour is dulled by the wood but, for this purpose, the effect is as good as that obtained with the proper dye.

Cellulose Paints

A spray canister of car paint was used to produce a glossy red dial for the Teddy Bear clock (page 28). If this finish is adopted, cellulose-based sanding sealers and cellulose thinners, which are available from model shops, will be needed both for priming the hardboard and for cleaning the brushes.

Sheet for Stencils

Full-size patterns are included for constructors who prefer to stencil numerals on to the larger dials (pages 30 and 34). Stencils can be cut from the thin acetate sheet stocked by model shops, and a fine felt-tipped pen can be used to trace the numerals on to its shiny surface. High-impact polystyrene sheet, a milky-white translucent material, is sold by some model shops as 'plastic building card' and constructors may find this easier to use than the acetate. Do not use these materials with cellulose-based paints: the solvents will dissolve them.

Rub-down Transfers and Self-adhesive Paper Labels

Rub-down transfers are used to apply numerals to the smaller dials. They are available in a wide range of styles and sizes, but remember that a clock face requires five '1s' and two '2s'. This may necessitate the purchase of more than one sheet to make up the sequence of twelve numbers. Self-adhesive plastic numerals are considered on page 10.

Eyes are cut from self-adhesive paper labels. Labels and rub-down transfers can be bought at most stationers.

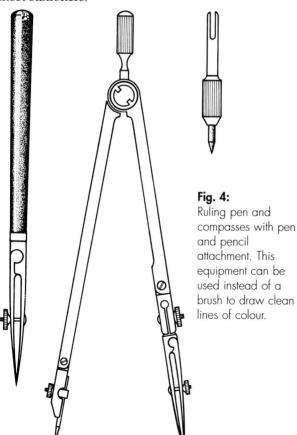

Fig. 4:
Ruling pen and compasses with pen and pencil attachment. This equipment can be used instead of a brush to draw clean lines of colour.

EQUIPMENT FOR APPLYING THE FINISHES

The clocks are comparatively small and the finishes are best applied with artists' rather than decorators' brushes. The following brushes and sundry items are suggested:

1 flat hog's-hair brush, 1½ in (38 mm), for applying the emulsion paint primer to hardboard sheets

2 flat water-colour brush, ½ in (13 mm) or 1 in (25 mm), for applying large areas of colour and the sealing varnish. A brush formed from synthetic filaments is suitable for this purpose

3 No. 6 and No. 2 water-colour brushes. Brushes formed from synthetic filaments are suitable, but make sure they draw to a point when wet

4 a piece of synthetic sponge for stippling difficult colours.

5 small stencil brush (only required if numerals are to be applied in this way). A child's cheap paintbrush with the bristles trimmed flat about ¼ in (6 mm) above the ferrule can work well

6 palette or small containers for mixing and diluting the colours. Inexpensive porcelain egg cups are ideal

7 low-tack masking tape

Useful but Non-essential Items

Fragmenting the dials into basic shapes eliminates most of the need for careful brushwork, but a few of the designs involve some colouring to drawn outlines. A draughtsman's ruling pen will ensure perfect results in most of these cases, and a ruling pen attachment in a pair of draughtsman's compasses will greatly ease the colouring of the rainbow (page 51). These items are illustrated in Fig. 4, and guidance on their use is given in the next chapter.

The inexpensive sets of ruling pens and compasses, which can be bought from some stationers, will probably be good enough for this purpose. Draughtsman's supply shops retail the professional, and more expensive, versions of the equipment.

2 CONSTRUCTING AND FINISHING THE CLOCKS

Colouring and finishing are brought to a stage of near completion before the final assembly of the dial parts. The step-by-step guidance which follows therefore embraces all aspects of the work, from gathering the materials and components together to hanging the completed clock on the wall.

Two of the dials involve finishing techniques that differ from the rest (Teddy Bear and Duck and Ducklings, pages 28 and 32). These alternative finishes are described on pages 25 and 26.

CONSTRUCTION AND FINISHING

Getting Started

1 Obtain the movement and hands, and all the materials needed to construct the clock. Any slight changes to accommodate a movement of different manufacture can then be considered before work begins.

Insert a battery, fit a second hand to the movement and check that it is working. This is particularly important in the case of pendulum movements which are to be modified, as any tampering with the unit will, quite understandably, void the guarantee. Very little power is drawn by the mechanism and the pendulum action takes a while to develop, but after a few seconds the plastic arm should respond to the impulses and begin to oscillate rapidly.

More than fifty quartz movements were purchased for making both this clock collection and the clocks featured in an earlier book, and they were all completely free from defects.

Priming the Hardboard

2 Dilute the white emulsion paint with water until it has a free-flowing, creamy consistency, then apply it to the smooth face of the hardboard and brush it out evenly.

Oily residues from the manufacturing process may prevent the paint flowing evenly. If this happens, wipe the board with a cloth dampened with water containing a little washing-up liquid.

When this first coat has dried (after about 15 minutes in a warm room), apply another coat. The dark surface of the hardboard will still be ghosting through, but more coats have to be applied later and the important point is to have the paint flowing freely enough to dry without brushmarks.

Transferring the Pattern to the Board

3 Using a sharp HB pencil and draughtsman's tracing paper, trace the full-size pattern of the dial. Cross-mark the centre points of the movement spindle hole and any eye sockets carefully, and use a straight edge when tracing centre lines. The full-size patterns for most of the symmetrical dials have been reproduced up to the centre line only. To obtain the other half of the design, simply turn the tracing paper over.

4 Decide how the parts are to be laid out on the board, lay the tracing paper, pencil-side down, in its first position, and secure it with small pieces of masking tape. Go over the required section of the design again with a sharp pencil; this will transfer some of the graphite from the original tracing on to the white surface of the hardboard. Mark the centres of eye sockets and spindle holes with particular care and, again, use a straight edge to transfer the centre line.

Turn the tracing paper over, align it carefully with the centre line, secure it to the board, and transfer the other half of the design.

5 Repeat this procedure for the various layers which make up the dial, always marking the centre line to aid alignment. In the case of parts which are not handed, pencil will, of course, have to be applied to the back of the tracing paper before the pattern can be transferred.

This technique eliminates the need for carbon paper, which is best avoided as pigments from it can bleed through subsequent layers of paint to appear on the finished surface.

6 Identify the centre points of any circular cuts and use the compasses to re-draw lines transferred freehand. Go over faint lines and clean up any defects; it is better to correct imperfections with a pencil now rather than to try and do so later with the saw.

Cutting Out the Parts

7 Use the fretsaw to cut out any irregular-shaped hardboard and $1/16$ in (1.5 mm) thick plywood parts. Always keep the saw kerf (the slot formed by the saw blade) on the waste side of the pencil line.

The saw is operated with its frame tucked under the arm, and the hardboard or plywood is moved and fed on to the blade rather than the saw being steered in different directions. Sit at a comfortable height in relation to the work, keep the saw vertical and the blade moving evenly up and down for a distance of about 2 in (50 mm) (see Fig. 5). Do not force the sawing action; take things steadily and give the blade a chance to cut its way through the sheet.

Drill blade-entry holes in eye sockets, ears and such like. One end of the fretsaw blade will, of course, have to be released from the frame, threaded through the entry hole and re-fixed before

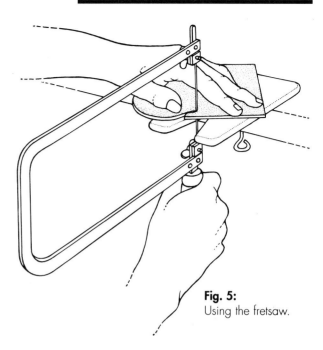

Fig. 5:
Using the fretsaw.

these apertures can be formed. Guidance on fitting a blade in the frame is given on page 12. If a $3/8$ in (10 mm) bit or drill is not available, the hole for the movement spindle will have to be made with the fretsaw.

8 Continuous straight cuts are best made with a dovetail or back saw (see Fig. 3, page 12). This saw can also be used for the preliminary removal of areas of waste and to cut the marked out sheets into smaller, more manageable pieces.

9 The modelling knife can be used to cut parts from $1/32$ in (0.8 mm) or $1/64$ in (0.4 mm) plywood. The Stanley knife is best for making straight cuts in $1/16$ in (1.5 mm) plywood, with the steel ruler guiding the blade.

Cleaning up Sheet Parts

10 Use files to correct outlines and smooth curves in hardboard and thicker plywood parts, then finish the edges with abrasive paper. The fretsaw cuts quickly and cleanly and, provided reasonable care has been taken, very little finishing will be required. Smooth straight-cut edges by applying the part to a sheet of abrasive paper laid on a flat surface. Use a round file to clean up, and enlarge if necessary, the hole for the movement spindle.

If intricate shapes start to fray during the cleaning up process, rub in a little adhesive, squeeze the layers together, and allow the edge to harden before proceeding.

Making Eyelids

11 Form eyelids from plastic wood built up on a ¹⁄₃₂ in (0.8 mm) or ¹⁄₆₄ in (0.4 mm) plywood mount. The mounting pieces are shaped to the lower profile of the eyelid and extend behind the face to give the necessary support. Fig. 6, together with Fig. 55 on page 63, makes the arrangement clear. Thin plywood mounts are desirable as they enable the moving eyes to be located close behind the face for best effect.

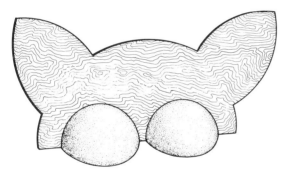

Fig. 6:
Plastic wood eyelids built up on a plywood mount which has been extended to form the inner-ear areas.

Use the hardboard body part as a template when marking out the position of the eyes and, where necessary, the profile of the head on the plywood (the mount sometimes extends upwards to form the inner-ear areas). This will ensure a perfect fit.

The two clocks featured on pages 119 and 123 have eyelids above fixed eyes. Here the plywood mount overlaps the entire eye socket and carries the eye parts as well as the eyelid.

Plastic wood applied in this thickness has to be left overnight in a warm place to harden. When hard, it can easily be carved with a modelling knife, and the correct shape is quickly established by removing fine shavings until the curved line of the eye socket, already pencilled on to the mount, is exposed.

It is unlikely that a perfect pair of eyelids will be obtained with the first application of plastic wood. After the initial carving, lift any low spots and smooth out defects with a further appliction of the material. This thinner layer will harden quite quickly and abrasive paper can then be used to refine the shape further. Repeat the process until the eyelids are smooth and well formed.

Making Beaks and Noses

12 Form Chuckaloo Tutu's beak (page 89) by building up plastic wood on a piece of thin plywood. Cut the plywood to the profile of the base of the beak, then proceed as described in 11, above.

Noses for Tom and Jenny and the Mad Mouser (pages 60 and 66) were carved from fine-grained wood, files and abrasive paper being used for the final shaping and finishing. If preferred, these items can be made from plastic wood by adopting the technique used to produce Tutu's beak.

A wood or plastic ball is used for Coco the Clown's nose. This is described fully on page 42.

Preparing the Parts for Colouring

13 Brush away all dust from the parts and apply three or four coats of the thinned white emulsion. Use garnet paper between applications to smooth any raised grain on plywood and any remaining roughness on hardboard parts.

Hold small parts with tweezers and apply the primer with the flat water-colour brush; this will make the process less messy. Put the parts on a sheet of polythene, rather than newspaper, to dry.

Surfaces should now be an even white and paper-smooth. If brush marks remain after the paint has dried, the emulsion has not been thinned sufficiently and therefore a little more water should be added.

Plastic numerals and metal clock hands can be coloured with poster paints if they are first given two coats of the white emulsion primer. Take care when priming the clock hands to avoid any paint flowing into the hour-hand collet.

Colouring the Parts

14 Add a little water to the poster colour to bring it to a thick, creamy consistency. It should brush on easily while still retaining its obliterating power. Different manufacturers' colours vary, but only a small amount of water is usually needed.

When paints are being mixed, be sure to make enough of each colour to complete the job, including any pendulum bob, numerals or hands which are to be painted in the same colour. It is virtually impossible to duplicate colours obtained in this way.

Always add small amounts of strong colour to white when mixing paler shades, *not* white to the strong colour. This method of working avoids the mixing of too much paint before the desired shade is obtained.

15 Transfer any drawn outlines to the parts by means of the technique described in 4 above. Most of the parts are a single colour, but a few include painted details; e.g. the clouds, distant hills and pathway on the Over the Rainbow clock (page 56) and the sun rays on the Ocean Liner clock (page 93).

16 Apply the poster colours to the primed hardboard and plywood. Use the ½ in (13 mm) or 1 in (25 mm) water-colour brush for larger areas and the No. 6 brush for small items. Brush the paint evenly over the parts, not forgetting to cover the edges. One coat is usually sufficient, but if there is any hint of the white primer ghosting through, apply another coat when the first is thoroughly dry. Provided the brush is not worked too vigorously, the second coat will not disturb the first.

Most colours change slightly on drying, and difficulty can be experienced getting an even finish with strong greens and some blues. Use a small piece of synthetic sponge to stipple on a second coat if this problem is encountered.

17 Details of an optional colour-shading technique are given on page 24. If the dial parts are to receive this treatment, it must be applied before the application of any varnish.

18 If the colour scheme or its execution are considered unsatisfactory, hold the parts under the tap and wash away the poster paint. The white emulsion primer is not water-soluble after it has dried and it will be exposed intact, ready for the second attempt.

This ability to wash away a poor colouring job and have another try makes the painting process very easy to master.

Preliminary Varnishing

19 Although not absolutely essential, it is a good idea to give the parts a first coat of varnish before they are assembled. This protects the rather vulnerable poster colours from damage while they are being handled.

Stir the varnish thoroughly to disperse the matting agent, then use the ½ in (13 mm) or 1 in (25 mm) water-colour brush to apply a thin, even coat to the painted parts, taking care to ensure that the edges are covered.

The application of the varnish will darken the colours initially, but when it dries (after about 4 hours in a warm room), the original colours will be restored and it will be difficult to tell that it has been applied. What looks like a milky-white film may appear on some bright colours (particularly purple). This is caused by the matting agent in the varnish being retained on the surface. The effect will disappear when further coats of varnish are applied later.

Leave the parts to dry overnight before proceeding to the next stage.

Assembling the Dial and Pendulum Bob Parts

20 Glue the parts together with balsa cement. Use the adhesive carefully and sparingly; if it smears or squeezes on to exposed areas, it will spoil the finish. Use large paper clips to hold the parts together until the adhesive hardens, inserting a slip of card under the jaws to protect the clock face.

Balsa cement can be applied to the emulsion-painted surface of the board (or to hidden patches of colour or varnish). The bonding of the various materials is so strong that the face of the hardboard would be torn away if an attempt were made to separate the layers, so make sure the parts are correctly positioned before the adhesive begins to harden.

Applying Numerals

21 Rub-down transfer and painted plastic numerals should be applied at this stage. Trace the position of the numerals from the relevant illustration and use this as a guide to apply numerals to the dial.

Gold-effect plastic numerals and markers are best stuck down after the final varnishing. Guidance on stencilling numerals is given on page 26.

Final Varnishing

22 Apply two more thin coats of varnish, as described in 19 above. This will provide a good degree of protection to the poster colours and the rub-down transfer or painted plastic numerals.

The construction of the dial and any pendulum bob is now complete.

PENDULUMS AND MOVING PARTS

Attaching Conventional Pendulum Bobs

A rear view of a pendulum bob, hardboard rod and the wire hook which attaches the assembly to the plastic arm on the movement, is given in Fig. 7 and is described on page 22.

Adapting the Pendulum Drive Unit

With the exception of the Octavia Octopus clock (page 80), all the clocks with moving eyes, or waving wings, flowers and balloons, require a top extension to the plastic pendulum arm on the quartz unit. This can be achieved by attaching the various moving parts directly to the plastic arm with pieces of brass wire, suitably bent and formed; the bluebird on the Over the Rainbow clock (page 56) is connected in this way.

A more robust method was, however, devised for the clocks which have larger or more elaborate systems of moving parts. The arrangement is depicted in Fig. 8, and illustrations throughout the book show how the basic design is altered to suit the different combinations of moving eyes, legs, tails and such like. It comprises a 1 in (25 mm) wide strip of 1/16 in (1.5 mm) plywood, secured to the plastic arm to extend it upwards. Platforms at the top and bottom of the strip enable eyes and tails to be securely fixed, and a larger surface area is created for attaching wires. Triangular plywood gussets stiffen the platforms. The plywood strip has to be spaced from the plastic arm; otherwise it would foul the projecting top suspension and the chiming chamber moulded on to the case of some quartz units. Construction should proceed as follows:

1 Mark out the parts on 1/16 in (1.5 mm) plywood, then cut them out with a Stanley knife. Use a steel

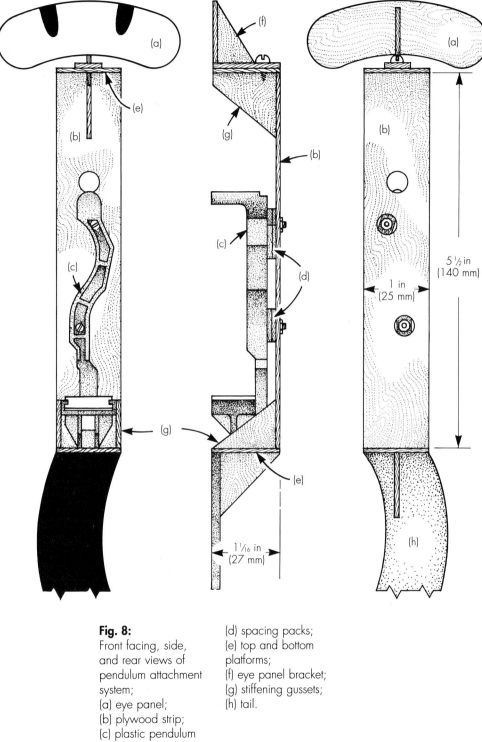

Fig. 7:
Hardboard pendulum
bob and rod with
wire hook.

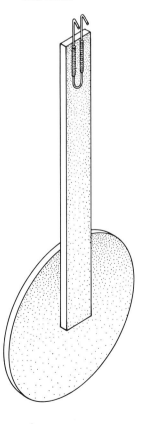

Fig. 8:
Front facing, side,
and rear views of
pendulum attachment
system;
(a) eye panel;
(b) plywood strip;
(c) plastic pendulum
arm;

(d) spacing packs;
(e) top and bottom
platforms;
(f) eye panel bracket;
(g) stiffening gussets;
(h) tail.

ruler to guide the knife and a try square or set square to ensure that right-angled corners are formed.

2 With the tip of a small screwdriver, lift the plastic retaining tag and slide the pendulum arm from its bearing. Drill ¹⁄₁₆ in (1.5 mm) holes through the web of the arm, near the top and bottom, then lay it on the plywood strip and mark the positions of the holes and the position of the top of the arm.

3 Drill ¼ in (6 mm) holes in the three positions. The nuts which secure the plywood packs to the plastic pendulum arm protrude through the holes and the larger diameter of the holes enables the position of the strip to be adjusted when it is cemented to the packs. The hole at the top of the arm gives access to the tag which retains the plastic pendulum arm on the movement.

4 Drill ¹⁄₁₆ in (1.5 mm) holes through the small plywood packing pieces and fix them to the plastic arm with small nuts and bolts or self-tapping screws. The packs are built up from two layers of ¹⁄₁₆ in (1.5 mm) plywood in order to obtain the required amount of clearance. Use balsa cement to attach the plywood strip to the packing pieces.

5 Cement the top and bottom platforms and the strengthening gussets to the plywood strip.
  This completes the pendulum modification.

Moving Eyes

Full-size patterns are included for the plywood panels which carry the moving eyes. Assembly and adjustment are described below:

1 Transfer the pattern for the eye panel onto ¹⁄₁₆ in (1.5 mm) or ¹⁄₃₂ in (0.8 mm) plywood and cut it out. Cut the mounting bracket parts from ¹⁄₁₆ in (1.5 mm) plywood and cement them together.

2 Fix the quartz movement behind the dial and slide the pendulum arm, complete with the plywood assembly, back on to its bearing. Locate

the eye panel behind the eye sockets and mark its position on the bracket. Glue the panel to the bracket, then attach the bracket to the top platform. Allow about ¹⁄₁₆ in (1.5 mm) clearance between the back of the head and the eye panel.
  The bracket can be glued or fixed by a self-tapping screw to the platform. Screw-fixing permits fine adjustment, and this is the arrangement shown in Fig. 8.

3 Draw the eyes on a self-adhesive paper label, colour them and cut them out. Holding them with tweezers, pass them though the eye sockets and locate them on the support panel. Their chosen position has quite an effect on facial expression and they are best stuck down with the pendulum mounted on its hanger.

Moving Stars, Birds, Balloons and Flowers

The stars, birds, balloons and flowers which wave and sway above the dials are connected to the pendulum assemblies by lengths of wire. Prepare and attach the wire in the following way:

1 Cut the wire to length, bend it to the required shape, then clean the ends with abrasive paper. Smear balsa cement on to the ends.

2 Wrap cotton thread tightly around the ends for a distance of about 1 in (25 mm), then give the bindings a liberal application of balsa cement.

3 Use balsa cement to attach the prepared ends of wires to stars, balloons, and such like, and to the plywood strip on the pendulum assembly. Cementing a length of thread-wrapped brass tube to the plywood strip enables the wire to be unplugged when the clock is stored or in transit (see Fig. 27, page 44).

Pendulum Length and Weight

Very little power is developed by the pendulum drive unit and this imposes limits on the length of the pendulum and the weight of the moving parts. The maximum pendulum length stipulated for the 717 unit is 23½ in (600 mm), and the load on its knife-bearing must not exceed 4¼ oz (120 g).

The clock designs have been kept within these limits and the moving parts oscillate vigorously. The counterbalancing effect of the tail on the Mad Mouser clock (page 66) and the stars on the celestial clock (page 123) help to ensure a good amplitude of swing despite the greater weight of the moving parts on these clocks. The pendulum drive unit does, however, have difficulty overcoming the inertia of the heavier systems, and the moving parts should be gently swung by hand to start them. The impulses from the drive unit will then keep them in motion.

Make sure that eye panels, connecting wires and other moving parts do not chafe on the dial: the slightest impediment will stop the parts oscillating.

Removing the Wall-Hanger Moulding from the Pendulum Movement Case

The top plywood platform has to be kept close to the pendulum bearing for three of the clocks (Dancing Clown, page 47; Mad Mouser, page 66; and Chuckaloo Tutu, page 89) and this necessitates the removal of the plastic wall-hanger moulded on to the case of the 717 quartz movement. Wrap a duster around the movement and steady it against the work bench, then use the junior hacksaw to cut through the plastic hanger in the positions shown on the clock drawings. Hold the movement gently but firmly, taking care not to put any stress on the hand-drive spindles.

FIXING QUARTZ MOVEMENTS AND HANDS

Movement and hand fixing arrangements are shown in Fig. 9. Units retailed in the United Kingdom are fixed to the dial by means of a tubular screw which engages with threads in the case. In the USA, the hand-drive shafts pass through a threaded sleeve which carries a fixing nut. Rubber washers are supplied with the movements, and thicker washers, cut from hardboard, can be used to reduce the front projection of the hand-drive spindles, should this be required.

Long-spindle movements must be fitted to dials comprising a single layer of board at the centre and several layers at the rim in order to ensure sufficient clearance for the tips of the hands; e.g. the Over the Rainbow clock, (page 56); the Penguins clock (page 71); and the Valley of the

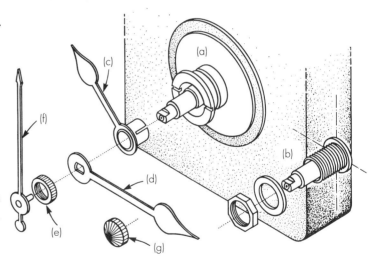

Fig. 9:
Quartz movement and hand fixings;
(a) European tubular screw fixing;
(b) American threaded bush and nut fixing;
(c) hour hand with collet;
(d) minute hand;
(e) open hand-fixing nut;
(f) second hand;
(g) blind hand-fixing nut used when a second hand is not fitted.

Dinosaurs clock (page 107). Washers have to be inserted beneath the tubular fixing screw in order to pack out the ⅛ in (3 mm) panel thickness. Fibre pipe-connector washers with a ⅜ in (10 mm) diameter hole can sometimes be obtained from plumbers' merchants. Failing this, wrap and cement a ⁵⁄₁₆ in (8 mm) wide strip of thin card around the screw to form a spacing sleeve.

In the case of the Penguins clock (page 71), even a long spindle movement will not provide sufficient clearance, and the hands have to be cranked slightly at the pivot. These arrangements are illustrated in Fig. 10.

Fix the hands with the movement set at the twelve o'clock position. Do not use excessive force to drive the hour hand on to its shaft; if necessary, insert a screwdriver blade into the splits in the collet and widen them very slightly. Lock the hands in position with a blind or closed nut when there is no second hand. An open nut is required when a second hand is fitted.

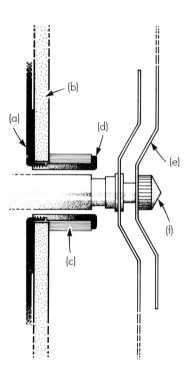

Fig. 10:
Fitting long-spindle movements to single-layer dials to ensure hand clearance at built-up rims;
(a) movement case;
(b) hardboard dial;
(c) washers or spacing sleeve;
(d) tubular fixing screw;
(e) hands cranked at pivot to further increase clearance above dial;
(f) hand-fixing nut.

OPTIONAL COLOUR-SHADING TECHNIQUE

The three-dimensional effect created by the layering of the dials can be enhanced by applying shadows and highlights to the parts.

The technique calls for a steady hand and some patience, but it can be mastered quite easily with a little practice and it gives a high degree of control over the shading process. Proceed as follows:

1 Apply the body colour to the parts, as described above, and allow it to dry thoroughly.

2 Using the No. 6 brush, apply a deeper tone of the body colour in a band along the edge of the part to be shaded.

3 Break up the edge of the band with dots of the deeper tone applied with the No. 2 brush.

4 Still using the No. 2 brush, apply smaller dots of the deeper tone along the uneven edge of the shading. Keep the dots quite close together where they adjoin the solid band of shading, but space them out more and more as they move further away from it.

For best results, the colour needs to be of a creamy consistency, and the brush loaded with just the right amount. If the shading is overdone in some areas, use the No. 2 brush to apply the original body colour over individual dots until the desired balance is obtained.

5 If highlights are required, mix a lighter tone of the body colour and dot it on with the No. 2 brush.

The various stages of the process are illustrated in Fig. 11 (page 26), and the colour photograph on page 27 gives a close-up view of the Teddy Bear's head and upper torso. Practise and experiment on cartridge paper. The technique can be mastered in less time than it takes to describe it.

USING RULING PENS

The ruling pens described and illustrated on page 15 can be loaded with thinned poster colour and used to draw perfectly even lines. Compasses with a pen attachment were used to produce the colour boundaries on the rainbow (see colour photographs on pages 14 and 57), and the outlines of the sun rays (see colour photograph on page 96) were drawn with a ruling pen. Constructors who wish to try this equipment should proceed in the following way:

1 Dilute the poster colour until it has the consistency of thin cream, then use the No. 6 brush to place a little between the blades of the pen.

2 Start the pen flowing by drawing it across the back of your hand. It may be necessary to adjust the wheel which sets the distance between the blades to get the flow started; a gap at the tip of about 1/16 in (1.5 mm) is about right for this purpose. If difficulty is experienced, the colour is probably too viscous and it should be thinned a little more.

3 Test the pen on cartridge paper, adjusting the blade setting wheel and the consistency of the colour until dense, even lines are produced; then rule the lines which will form colour boundaries on the dial parts.

Hold the pen vertically, or at a slight trailing angle, and clean the blades after drawing each line (residues of dried colour will prevent it from working). Make sure it is loaded with sufficient colour to complete a line at one pass as it is difficult to produce an imperceptible join.

4 When using compasses with a ruling pen attachment to draw the rainbow (page 57), secure the dial to a flat surface with low-tack masking tape and locate the centre point of the arc by trial and error. The pen attachment produces perfect edges to the bands of colour and the area between is filled in with the No. 2 brush.

ALTERNATIVE DIAL FINISHES

Different finishes were applied to the dials of the Teddy Bear (page 28) and the Duck and Ducklings (page 32) clocks. The procedures already described will produce excellent results, but guidance is given below for constructors who would like to try these alternative treatments.

Spray Cellulose Finish

Here the round dial is given a hard, bright, glossy finish. Proceed as follows:

1 Cut out the circles of hardboard for the dial and the pendulum bob, and form the hole for the movement spindle. Clean up the sawn edges, then remove any remaining blemishes with garnet (fine grade abrasive) paper.

2 Stir the cellulose-based sanding sealer thoroughly, adding cellulose thinners, as necessary, until a free-flowing consistency is obtained. Use the 1/2 in (13 mm) or 1 in (25 mm) flat water-colour brush to apply two or three coats of sealer to the hardboard. The solvents are extremely volatile and the sealer dries quickly. Keep the work area well-ventilated and remove any blemishes with garnet paper as each coat hardens.

3 Lay the dial and pendulum bob flat and supported above the work surface. Apply two or three coats of car spray paint, following the instructions printed on the canister.

Stain Finish

The plywood dial and pendulum bob of the Duck and Ducklings clock (page 32) are stained to make the swirling pattern of the grain resemble water. Proprietary wood dyes can be obtained for this purpose but, in view of the small quantity involved, coloured drawing ink makes an acceptable substitute. Cut out the plywood parts

  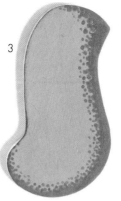  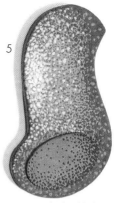

Fig. 11:
The various stages of the colour shading process:
(1) Apply the basic body colour.

(2) Apply a deeper tone of the body colour in a band along the edge to be shaded.

(3) Break up the edge of the band with dots of the deeper tone.

(4) Apply smaller dots of the deeper tone, keeping the dots close together where they adjoin the band of shading.

(5) Provide highlights by dotting in a lighter tone of the basic body colour.

and smooth them with garnet paper, then proceed as follows:

1 Moisten the surface of the plywood with a damp sponge and leave it to dry. This will raise any loose fibres which would otherwise be lifted when the ink is applied. Smooth the parts with garnet paper again.

2 Apply the ink liberally and evenly with the ½ in (13 mm) or 1 in (25 mm) water-colour brush. Leave the parts to dry overnight.

3 Give the stained parts two or three coats of matt varnish, all as described on page 19, using garnet paper to remove any blemishes after each coat has hardened.

STENCILLING NUMERALS

Although poster colours can be laid one on another without difficulty, the stippling action of a stencil brush can cause the base coat to soften and lift. This problem can be avoided by stencilling the numbers after the poster colour on the dial has been protected by one or two coats of varnish. When the varnish has dried, proceed as follows:

1 Use a fine felt-tipped pen to trace the numerals on to acetate sheet. The hour line and dial

circumference positions are given in Figs. 15 and 19 (pages 30 and 34). Trace these on to the stencil. They will be of help when the numerals are being positioned on the dial.

Cut out the numerals using a scalpel or a modelling knife with a pointed blade. Cover any mistakes with clear cellulose tape and cut again.

2 Lay the dial on a sheet of paper and secure it with small pieces of low-tack masking tape. Draw the hour lines on the paper around the circumference of the dial. (They can be traced from the clock pattern.)

3 Use the hour lines to position the stencil on the dial and hold it down with small pieces of masking tape. Work the brush gently when stippling the colour through. Use the poster colour straight from the jar, and remove any excess paint from the brush by dabbing it on a sheet of paper. A lightly loaded brush and a stiff paint consistency are essential; otherwise the colour would flow under the stencil.

4 Paint out the stencil ties and clean up any blurring of the outlines with the No. 2 brush. A moistened cotton bud is useful for removing any unwanted areas of colour.

5 Seal and protect the numerals with a further two coats of varnish.

Close-up of the face and upper torso of the Teddy bear
showing the optional colour shading.

3 NURSERY NOVELTIES

Teddy bears and ducks and ducklings are among the most comforting of the images associated with childhood. These two clocks, with their bright colours, big numerals and simple shapes, are clearly meant for the nursery. They are very easy to construct.

Fig. 12:
Teddy Bear.

TEDDY BEAR

The finished clock is shown in both the colour photograph (page 31) and Fig. 12. A full-size pattern for the bear is given in Fig. 13 opposite.

The bear shape is divided where the arms, legs and head are joined to the torso. This produces a more realistic effect and makes the optional colour-shading process easier to apply.

Construction

The step-by-step guidance given in Chapters 1 and 2 covers all aspects of the construction and finishing of this clock. Constructors who do not feel too confident about painting the paw and ear pads with the No. 2 brush might prefer to cut them from very thin – 1/32 in (0.8 mm) or 1/64 in (0.4 mm) – plywood and stick them in place after colouring. The nose and bow tie were applied in this way.

If the colour-shading process is attempted, note the disc of lighter colour, centred just beneath the nose, which includes the chin and touches the eyes. The close-up view in the colour photograph on page 27 shows this.

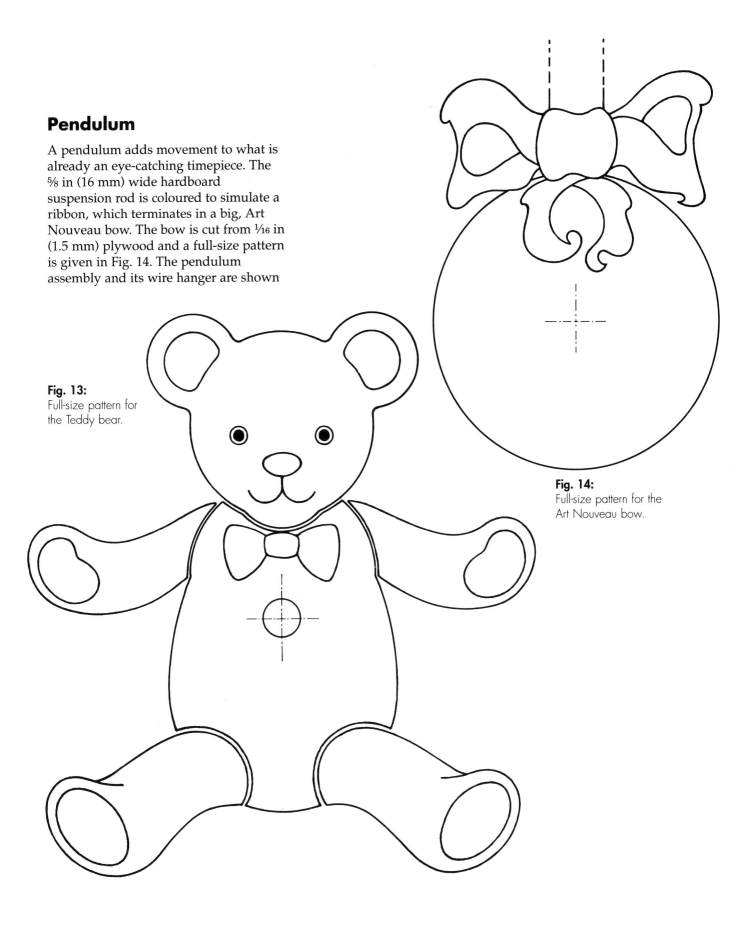

Pendulum

A pendulum adds movement to what is already an eye-catching timepiece. The ⅝ in (16 mm) wide hardboard suspension rod is coloured to simulate a ribbon, which terminates in a big, Art Nouveau bow. The bow is cut from 1/16 in (1.5 mm) plywood and a full-size pattern is given in Fig. 14. The pendulum assembly and its wire hanger are shown

Fig. 13:
Full-size pattern for the Teddy bear.

Fig. 14:
Full-size pattern for the Art Nouveau bow.

in Fig. 7 (page 21). A hardboard pack behind the knot in the bow lifts the ribbons clear of the bob. The bands of colour on the rod were defined with a ruling pen, but this is very much an optional feature.

Numerals

A full-size pattern for the ⅞ in (22 mm) high stencilled numerals is given in Fig. 15. Constructors who wish to avoid stencilling could use rub-down transfers or self-adhesive plastic numerals, but should take care not to make them smaller. With plastic numerals, either leave the gold finish and fit brass hands, or colour numerals and hands, all as described in Chapter 2. The Pisces clock shown in the colour photograph on page 76 has ⅞ in (22 mm) plastic numerals which have been coloured.

Colour Scheme

Dial and pendulum bob bright red

Bear body colour mid yellow (add a little orange if there is no shading)

Paw and ear pads and the eyes suede (white plus brown)

Eye pupils, nose and mouth brown

Bow tie, pendulum bow and pendulum rod mid blue (ultramarine plus turquoise, white dots on bow tie)

Hands and numerals lime green (white plus green)

Optional Shading

Bear shading orange

Bear highlights pale yellow (white plus mid yellow)

Lighter tones on pendulum rod and bow turquoise

Fig. 15: Full-size pattern for the ⅞ in (22 mm) numerals. Hour lines and circumference segments are included to aid the positioning of the numerals on the dial.

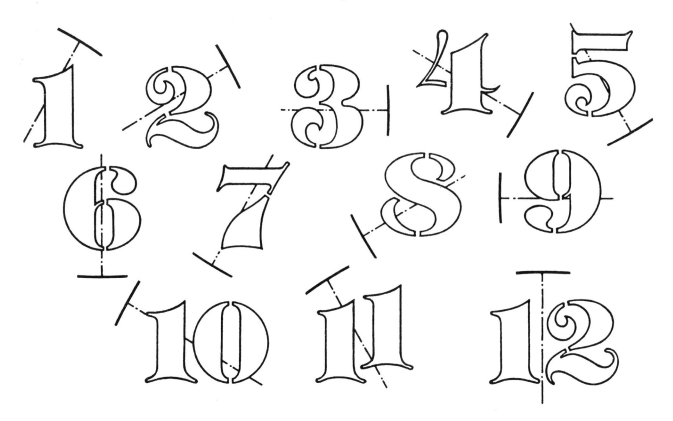

Materials and Parts

Dial board, bear, pendulum rod and bob hardboard, 18 × 10 in (460 × 255 mm)

Bow tie, nose, paw and ear pads 1/32 in (0.8 mm) or 1/64 in (0.4 mm) thick plywood, 4 × 3 in (100 × 75 mm)

Bow on pendulum 1/16 in (1.5 mm) plywood, 4 × 3 in (100 × 75 mm)

Stencil thin acetate or plastic sheet, 11½ × 8 in (295 × 210 mm)

Medium spindle quartz movement with blind hand-fixing nut

Hands 3⅞ in (98 mm), brass for colouring

Balsa cement; 3 in (75 mm) of 1/32 in (0.8 mm) brass wire; cotton thread; cellulose-based sanding sealer; cellulose thinners; paints and varnish

Teddy Bear

DUCK AND DUCKLINGS

The finished clock is shown in the colour photograph and Fig. 16. A full-size pattern for the duck and ducklings group is given in Fig. 17, and the location of the movement spindle hole has been included to make it easier to position the arrangement on the dial. Dividing the group into individual birds avoids linework with the brush and also gives a more pleasing effect. The pattern for the duck on the optional pendulum is shown in Fig. 18.

Construction

Full details are given in Chapters 1 and 2. The dial and pendulum bob are cut from ³⁄₁₆ in (5 mm) plywood and stained. If light coloured plywood with a distinct, swirling grain cannot be obtained, use hardboard and colour it blue.

Pendulum

The pendulum bob is built up from a hardboard duck stuck to a plywood disc. A ³⁄₈ in (10 mm) wide hardboard rod suspends it from the quartz movement. Typical pendulum details are illustrated in Fig. 7 on page 21.

Numerals

Comments made on page 30 about numerals and hands for the Teddy Bear clock apply to this timepiece also. The stencilled numerals are reproduced in Fig. 19 (page 34). At 1 in (25 mm) high they are bolder than those applied to the Teddy Bear clock.

Colour Scheme

Plywood dial and bob blue (cobalt blue drawing ink)

Hardboard dial and bob mid blue (ultramarine plus turquoise)

Ducks and pendulum rod white (emulsion paint primer)

Duck beaks orange

Duck eyes black

Numerals and hands yellow (mid yellow plus white)

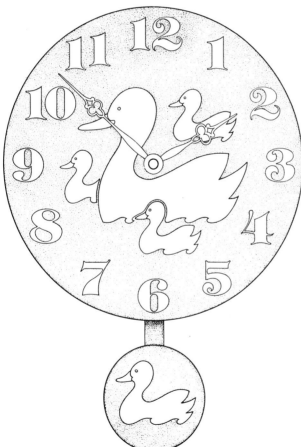

Fig. 16:
Duck and Ducklings.

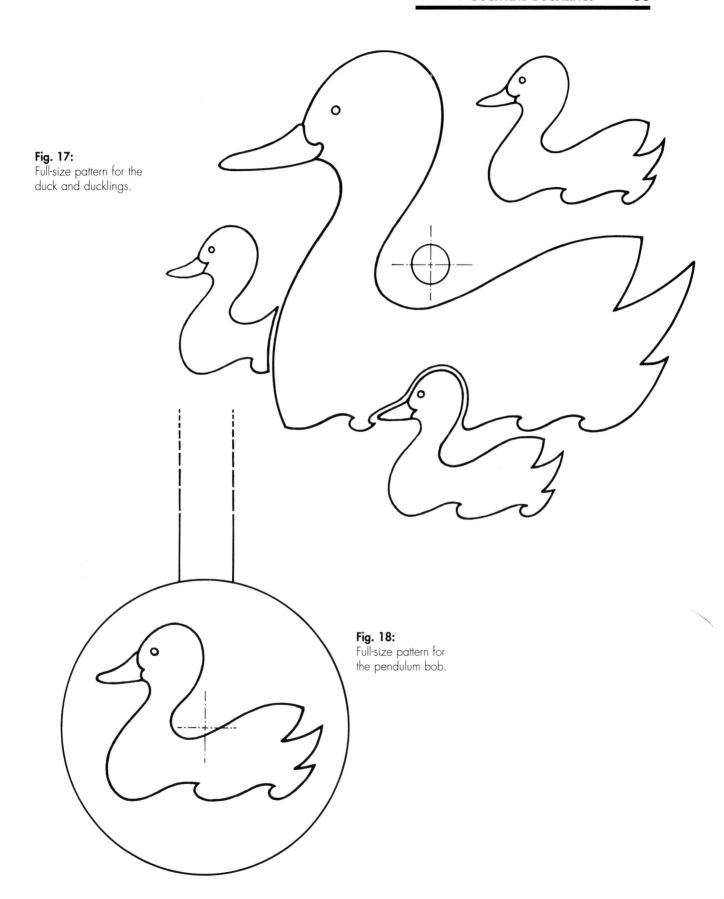

Fig. 17:
Full-size pattern for the
duck and ducklings.

Fig. 18:
Full-size pattern for
the pendulum bob.

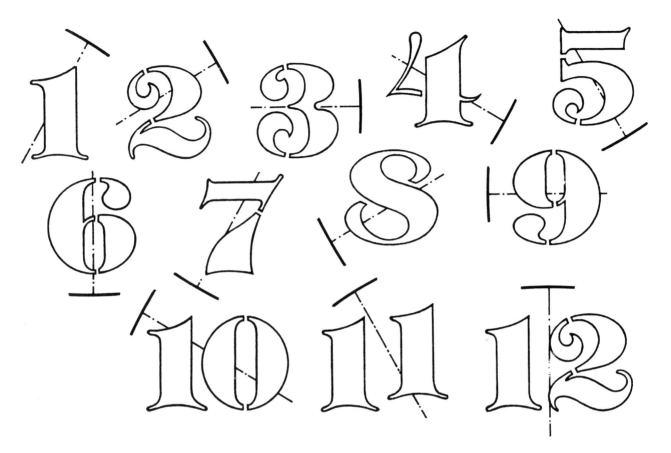

Fig. 19:
Full-size pattern for the 1 in (25 mm) numerals. Hour lines and circumference segments help to position the numerals on the dial.

Materials and Parts

Dial and pendulum bob ³⁄₁₆ in (5 mm) thick plywood, 12 × 10 in (305 × 255 mm)

Ducks and pendulum rod hardboard, 7 × 6 in (180 × 150 mm)

Dial, ducks and pendulum parts (hardboard version) hardboard, 18 × 10 in (460 × 255 mm)

Stencil thin acetate or plastic sheet, 11½ × 8 in (295 × 210 mm)

Medium spindle quartz movement with blind hand-fixing nut

Hands 3⅞ in (98 mm), brass for colouring

Balsa cement; 3 in (75 mm) length of ¹⁄₃₂ in (0.8 mm) brass wire; cotton thread; cobalt blue drawing ink; paints and varnish

4 BEARS IN THE AIR

The high prices collectors are prepared to pay for tired old Teddy bears confirm that affection for the toy lingers on beyond childhood. Aficionados may find these slightly more intricate clocks of interest; if not for themselves, then as gifts for their children or grandchildren.

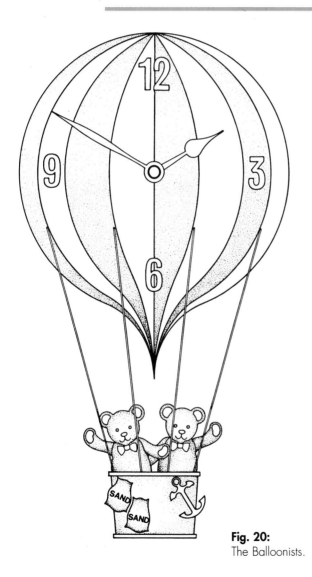

Fig. 20:
The Balloonists.

THE BALLOONISTS

The clock is shown in both the colour photograph (page 38) and Fig. 20. A full-size pattern for the balloon is given in Fig. 21 (opposite), and for the bears and basket in Fig. 22 opposite. Basket trim, ballast sacks and an anchor provide touches of detail, and an optional second hand would add movement to this brightly coloured timepiece.

Construction

The balloon is built up in four layers and the only precise brushwork is to the line which passes through the centre of the dial. A ruling pen can be used to produce a perfect boundary between the colours (page 25), or the top layer can be cut on the centre line to eliminate this tricky colouring, if preferred. Square apertures are cut in the first two layers of the balloon to accommodate the movement case, and a medium spindle-length unit can be installed.

The basket trims and anchor are cut from 1/16 in (1.5 mm) plywood; all other parts are of hardboard. Cement the brass suspension wires into $\frac{1}{32}$ in (0.8 mm) holes drilled into the top edge of the basket. Bend the other ends of the wires at right angles and cement them into holes drilled into the balloon.

The bears in this design are too small for their paw and ear pads to be cut from plywood, and these features have to be added using the No. 2 brush.

Numerals

The layered construction gives this dial an uneven perimeter and only four numerals were applied with the No. 2 brush, different colours being used to contrast with the dial. Constructors may wish to substitute four $\frac{5}{8}$ in (16 mm), self-adhesive plastic numerals. The gold finish would match the brass hands and a set of numerals of this type has been included in the parts list.

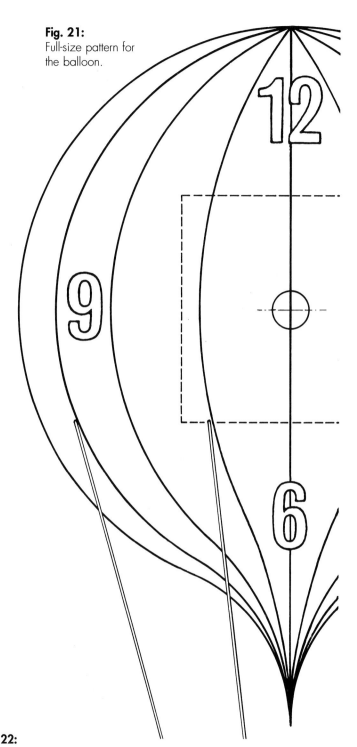

Fig. 21:
Full-size pattern for the balloon.

Fig. 22:
Full-size pattern for the bears and basket.

The Balloonists

Colour Scheme

Balloon bright red, yellow, green and blue (mix ultramarine and turquoise for the blue)

Basket bright red

Basket trim blue (mix as above)

Bear Light orange (yellow plus orange)

Bear features Brown

Bear ear and paw pads suede (white plus brown)

Bow ties red and blue (white dots)

Sand bags light brown (yellow plus brown)

Anchor orange

Optional Shading

Bears light brown (orange plus brown)

Sand bags brown

Materials and Parts

Balloon, basket, sand bags and bears hardboard, 15 × 12 in (380 × 305 mm)

Basket trim and anchor 1/16 in (1.5 mm) thick plywood, 2½ × 1 in (65 × 25 mm)

Medium spindle quartz movement (an open hand-fixing nut will be required if a second hand is fitted)

Hands 2½ in (65 mm), brass

Second hand (if required) 2¾ in (70 mm), brass

Numerals ⅝ in (16 mm), gold effect, self-adhesive plastic

Balsa cement; two 12 in (305 mm) lengths of 1/32 in (0.8 mm) brass wire; paints and varnish

CLOUD HOPPER

This madly swaying bear has left the picnic far behind. A benign sun peeps out from behind a dial of white clouds, and the complete timepiece is shown in both the colour photograph and Fig. 24 (page 40).

Construction

Full-size patterns for the dial and the bear-and-balloons pendulum are given in Figs. 23 (page 40) and 25 (page 41). Cutting out the fluffy clouds takes time, but the finished result is worth the effort. The clock is built up in four layers and the cloud near the three o'clock position is held off the back of the dial by small hardboard packs.

The sun's features and the detail on the bear require careful brushwork, but the shading on the clouds is easy to apply and greatly enhances the three-dimensional effect created by the layering.

Although the dial is only ⅛ in (3 mm) thick, a medium spindle-length movement should be fitted to ensure that the tip of the minute hand clears the clouds located at the edge of the dial.

Pendulum

The bear and balloons form the pendulum. The green balloon is attached to the red balloon's wire where it passes behind it, and the red and blue balloons

Cloud Hopper

are linked by a short wire: this keeps the
entire pendulum arrangement rigid.

The hook which engages with the
plastic arm on the quartz movement is
formed from brass wire, then bound
with thread and cemented behind the
red balloon. The hook must extend 1 in
(25 mm) above the top balloon to give
clearance beneath the clouds.

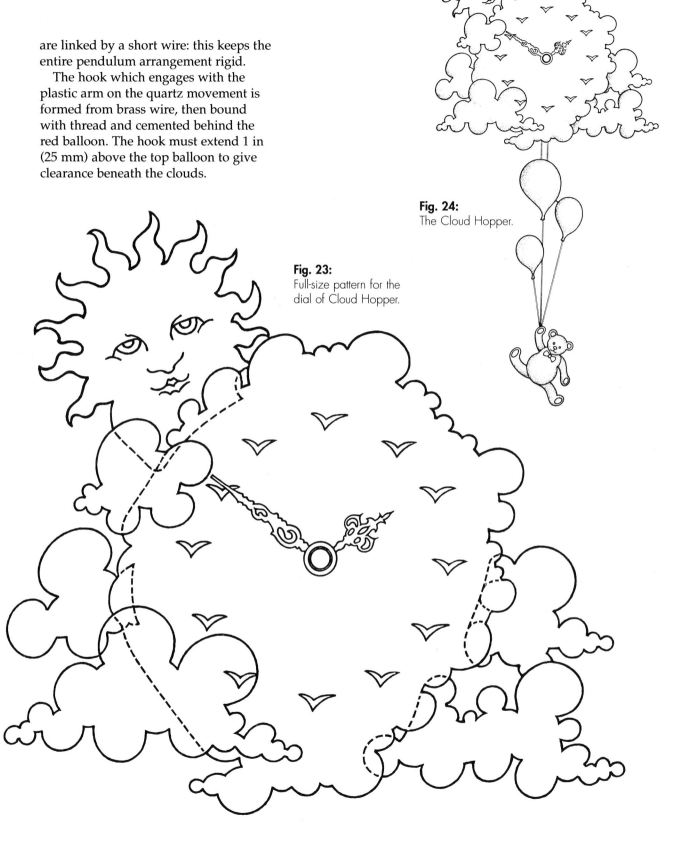

Fig. 24:
The Cloud Hopper.

Fig. 23:
Full-size pattern for the
dial of Cloud Hopper.

Hour Markers

Bluebirds were drawn on to the clouds with a No. 2 brush to act as hour markers, but ¼ in (6 mm) self-adhesive plastic markers, or rub-down transfer numerals, could be applied instead.

Colour Scheme

Clouds white (emulsion paint primer)

Hands, hour markers and shading on clouds pale blue (white plus turquoise)

Sun mid yellow

Sun's features bright red

Shading on sun orange

Balloons bright red, blue and green (mix ultramarine and turquoise for the blue)

Bear light orange (yellow plus orange)

Bear features brown

Bear ear and paw pads suede (white plus brown)

Bear shading brown (orange plus brown)

Materials and Parts

Clouds, sun, bear and balloons hardboard, 12 × 6 in (305 × 150 mm)

Medium spindle length quartz movement with blind hand-fixing nut

Hands 1⅜ in (36 mm), brass for colouring

Hour markers ¼ in (6 mm) self-adhesive plastic (if required)

Balsa cement; two 12 in (305 mm) lengths of ¹⁄₃₂ in (0.8 mm) brass wire; cotton thread; paints and varnish

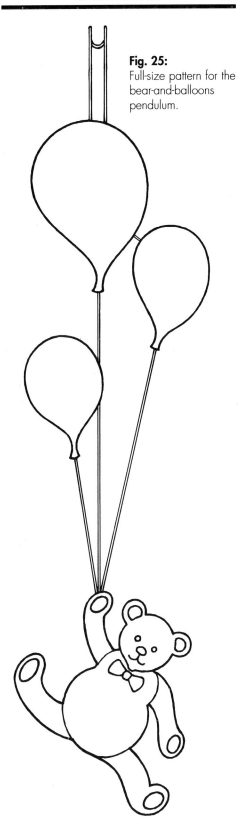

Fig. 25: Full-size pattern for the bear-and-balloons pendulum.

5 CLOWN CLOCKS

The painted faces and ridiculous clothes of circus clowns feature in the two clocks described in this chapter. Waving flowers and balloons, twitching bow ties and wagging legs all add to the comic effect.

COCO THE CLOWN

This clock is illustrated in the colour photograph opposite with front and rear views in Figs. 26 and 27 (page 44). A full-size pattern for the face and hat is given in Fig. 28, for the flower in Fig. 29, and for the bow tie in Fig. 30 (all page 45). The flower and tie wag from side to side, powered by the pendulum drive on the quartz movement.

Construction

The various hardboard and plywood parts and the nose ball are shown separately in Fig. 31 (page 46). The clock is a little more complicated than those considered so far, and this illustration should help clarify the method of assembly. The thin plywood which forms the hat band also forms the under-brim area, and the boundary between red and blue lies beneath the brim piece, thus avoiding the need for careful brushwork.

The rear view of the clock, Fig. 27, shows the connections between the flower, the bow tie, and the plywood strip attached to the plastic pendulum arm. (The modifications to the quartz movement are described in Chapter 2, but plywood platforms are not required here.) With this arrangement, small stand-off blocks have to be glued behind the dial to keep the moving parts clear of the wall and the plastic hanging bracket cannot be used. Instead, a plywood strip is fixed between the two upper blocks to carry a picture hanger. Use screws to fix this strip so that it can be removed to give access to the pendulum-retaining clip at the top of the movement case.

Pieces of rectangular brass tube, bound with thread and then cemented to the plywood pendulum strip, act as sockets for the wires which connect the flower and bow tie and enable these parts to be removed when the clock is stored. Bending the ends of the wires into a long, narrow 'U', and the use of rectangular tube, prevent the parts rotating.

The brass socket for the flower is cranked forward to bring it just behind the crown of the hat. The thicker brass wire which carries the bow tie is likewise bent to bring it into line with the clown's chin.

Bound wire is used to connect the petals to the centre of the flower. This creates a delicate effect, but constructors

Fig. 26:
Coco the Clown.

Fig. 27:
Rear view of clock;
(a) lengths of brass
tubing used as sockets
for the flower and
bow-tie wires;
(b) pendulum
attachment strip;
(c) wall-hanger strip;
(d) wall stand-off
blocks;
(e) movement.

who do not want to bother with this can cement the tips of the petals behind the centre disc.

Form a shallow hole in the nose ball, just large enough to accept a blind hand-fixing nut as a tight push fit, and screw the nose on to the hand shaft.

Numerals

Gold finish, self-adhesive ⅝ in (16 mm) plastic numerals add glitter to the dial and match the brass hands. The number '11' has to be cut down a little with a modelling knife in order to accommodate the curls.

Colour Scheme

Flower petals and area around mouth white (emulsion paint primer)

Flower centre orange

Crown of hat blue (turquoise)

Hat band bright red

Hat brim mid blue (ultramarine plus turquoise)

Under hat brim blue (turquoise)

Eyebrows and curls orange

Face skin tone (white plus traces of yellow, red and brown)

Eyes brown

Nose bright red

Ruff pale yellow (white plus yellow)

Bow tie blue (turquoise with white spots)

Optional Shading

Flower centre and eyebrows red

Crown of hat and bow tie mid blue (ultramarine plus turquoise)

Fig. 28:
Full-size pattern for
the dial.

Fig. 29:
Full-size pattern for
the flower.

Fig. 30:
Full-size pattern for
the bow tie.

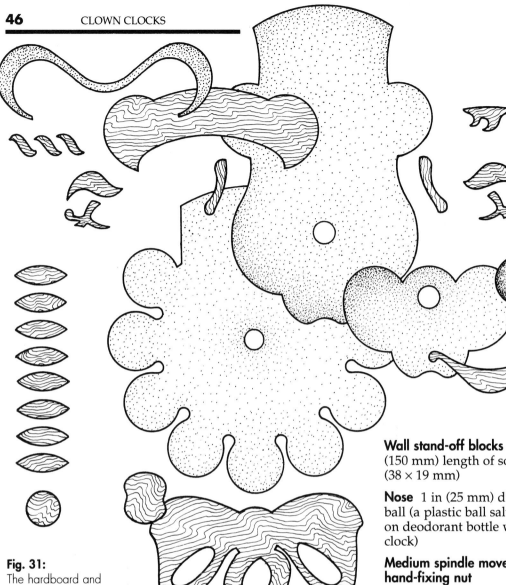

Fig. 31:
The hardboard and plywood parts which make up the clock.

Materials and Parts

Ruff, face and crown of hat, hat brim and area around mouth hardboard, 12 × 9 in (305 × 230 mm)

Curls, eyebrows, ears, flower parts, pendulum attachment strip and packs ¹⁄₁₆ in (1.5 mm) thick plywood, 6 × 6 in (150 × 150 mm)

Hat band and underbrim area, eyes and mouth ¹⁄₃₂ in (0.8 mm) or ¹⁄₆₄ in (0.4 mm) thick plywood, 6 × 3 in (150 × 75 mm)

Wall stand-off blocks four out of a 6 in (150 mm) length of softwood, 1½ × ¾ in (38 × 19 mm)

Nose 1 in (25 mm) diameter wooden ball (a plastic ball salvaged from a roll-on deodorant bottle was used for this clock)

Medium spindle movement with blind hand-fixing nut

Hands 2½ in (65 mm), brass

Numerals ⅝ in (16 mm) gold finish, self-adhesive plastic

Balsa cement; 6 in (150 mm) of ³⁄₆₄ in (1 mm) brass wire (for bow tie hanger); 12 in (305 mm) of ¹⁄₃₂ in (0.8 mm) brass wire (for flower); two small bolts for pendulum attachment strip, ¹⁄₁₆ in (1.5 mm) maximum diameter × ⅜ in (10 mm) long, complete with nuts; 6 in (150 mm) of rectangular brass tube ³⁄₁₆ × ¹⁄₁₆ in (4.5 × 1.5 mm); two ⅜ in (10 mm) No. 6 brass screws; brass picture hanger with two small self-tapping screws; cotton thread; paints and varnish

DANCING CLOWN WITH BALLOONS

This clock is shown in the colour photograph and in Figs. 32 (page 48) and 36 (page 50). Full-size patterns are given in Figs. 33, 34 and 35 (all on page 49). The pendulum drive unit waves the red balloon and also wags the legs and lower torso.

Construction

The rear view (Fig. 36) shows the plywood strip attached to the plastic pendulum arm, the wood blocks which space the clock from the wall, and the hanging arrangements.

Space is more limited behind the head on this design, and the plastic hanger must be removed from the movement case (see Chapter 2) to provide clearance for the cranked brass wire which acts as the balloon string. Fitting a rectangular brass socket, as described earlier in this chapter, would permit the removal of the waving balloon when the clock is stored.

The legs and lower torso are cemented to the bottom platform on the plywood pendulum strip (there is no top platform with this clock). Allow about $\frac{1}{16}$ in (1.5 mm) clearance behind the dial balloon, and stiffen the connection with plywood gussets, all as shown in Fig. 36.

The dial balloon is held in place by the movement fixing screw and there is no need to cement it. The blue balloon is cemented to the back of the clown's head and the green balloon is attached to it by a short length of wire.

The head, face and features are built up in four layers. The 'exploded' view of the head, given in Fig. 37, should help to make the construction clear. The separate bow tie and the hand and hand packs are included in this illustration. The nose is a bead, cut in half, and the eyes are painted on to the face with the No. 2 brush.

Trousers and braces (suspenders in the USA) were cut from thin plywood, but constructors who feel sufficiently confident could paint these items in with a brush. Shirt and socks need careful brushwork, but the blue stripes could be omitted, if preferred, without detracting too much from the appearance of the clock.

Numerals

Rub-down transfer numerals, ⅜ in (10 mm) high, were applied to the dial.

Colour Scheme

Upper balloons bright red, blue and green (use ultramarine plus turquoise for the blue)

Dial balloon light yellow (mid yellow plus white)

Skull cap, hair, eyebrows, nose, mouth, clock hands, braces and shoes bright red (yellow spots on braces)

Face and hands skin tone (white plus traces of yellow, red and brown)

Eyes mid blue (mix as above)

Area around mouth white

Shirt and socks orange with blue stripes (mix blue as above)

Bow tie and trousers mid green (yellow spots on tie)

Fasteners on braces mid yellow

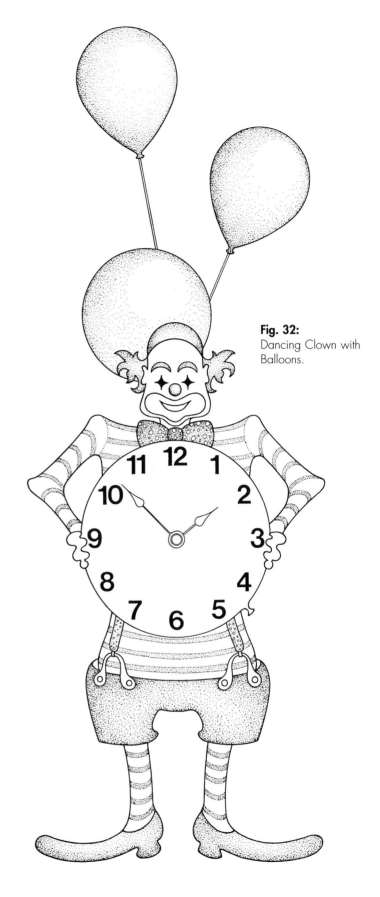

Fig. 32:
Dancing Clown with Balloons.

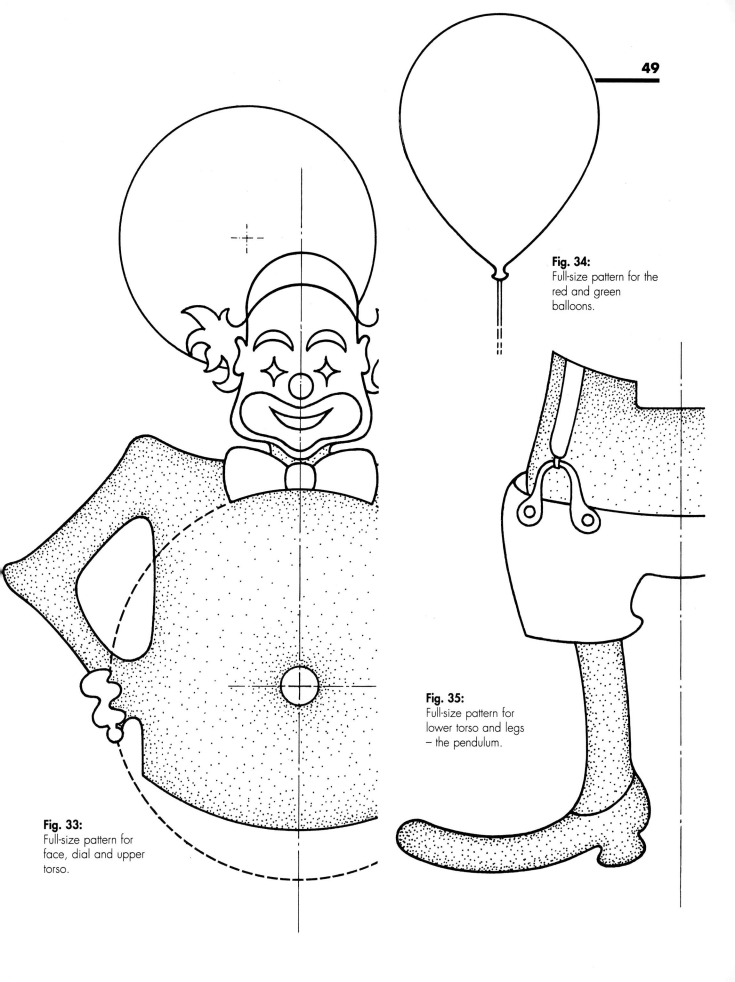

Fig. 34:
Full-size pattern for the
red and green
balloons.

Fig. 35:
Full-size pattern for
lower torso and legs
– the pendulum.

Fig. 33:
Full-size pattern for
face, dial and upper
torso.

Materials and Parts

Balloons, dial balloon, face, torso parts, hands and hand packs hardboard, 12 × 12 in (305 × 305 mm)

Skull cap, hair, eyebrows, bow tie, trousers; pendulum attachment strip, packs, platform and gussets 1/16 in (1.5 mm) thick plywood, 6 × 6 in (150 × 150 mm)

Area around mouth and braces 1/32 in (0.8 mm) or 1/64 in (0.4 mm) plywood, 3 × 2 in (75 × 50 mm)

Wall stand-off blocks four out of a 6 in (150 mm) length of softwood 1½ × ¾ in (38 × 19 mm)

Nose 7/16 in (11 mm) diameter wood or plastic bead, cut in half

Medium spindle quartz movement with blind hand-fixing nut

Hands 1⅝ in (41 mm), brass for colouring

Numerals ⅜ in (10 mm), rub-down transfer

Balsa cement; 18 in (460 mm) of 1/32 in (0.8 mm) brass wire; two small bolts for pendulum attachment, 1/16 in (1.5 mm) maximum diameter × ⅜ in (10 mm) long, complete with nuts; two ⅜ in (10 mm) No. 6 brass screws; brass picture hanger with two small self-tapping screws; cotton thread; paints and varnish

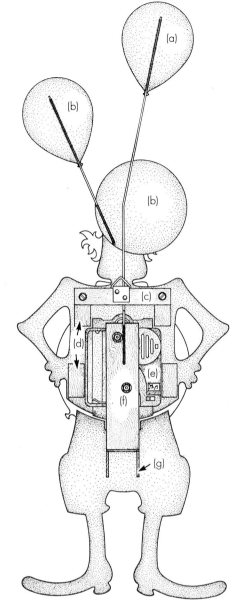

Fig. 36:
Rear view of dancing clown;
(a) moving balloon;
(b) fixed balloons;
(c) wall-hanger strip;
(d) wall stand-off blocks;
(e) movement;
(f) pendulum attachment strip;
(g) gussets.

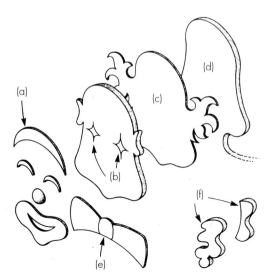

Fig. 37:
Head, face and hand parts; (a) features and skull cap; (b) eyes painted on to hardboard face; (c) plywood hair; (d) head; (e) bow tie; (f) hand and hand packing piece.

6 COUNTRY CLOCKS

With their blue skies, green meadows and distant hills, these two clocks have a strong pastoral theme.

Fig. 38:
March Hares.

MARCH HARES

Hares chase one another around the dial shown in the colour photograph on page 52 and Fig. 38. Full-size patterns for the hares are given in Fig. 39 (page 53), and for the rolling meadow in Fig. 40 (page 54).

Construction

The hardboard parts which make up the sweeping pattern of meadow and sky are cut out with the fretsaw and coloured before being reassembled on a backing disc of hardboard or plywood. Use a sponge to stipple on the green if difficulty is experienced obtaining an even finish with this colour.

The optional pendulum, shown full-size in Fig. 41 (page 55), is built up from hardboard and plywood parts which are also coloured before assembly.

Colour Scheme

Sky blue (turquoise), pale blue (white plus turquoise)

Meadow mid green, light green (yellow plus mid green)

Flowers orange, white

Hands white

Hare body grey (white with hints of black, red and brown)

Hare underbody pale grey (white plus body colour)

Optional Shading

Hare body darker mix of body colour

Hare underbody speckle with body colour

The dial colours are repeated on the pendulum (see the colour photograph) and a ruling pen can be used to define the bands of sky colour on the pendulum rod.

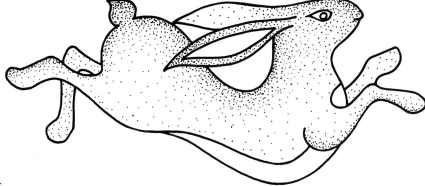

Materials and Parts

Dial, dial back plate, hares, pendulum bob and rod hardboard, 18 × 12 in (460 × 305 mm)

Pendulum sky and flower parts 1/16 in (1.5 mm) thick plywood, 3 × 2 in (75 × 50 mm)

Medium spindle quartz movement with blind hand-fixing nut

Hands 3⅞ in (98 mm), brass, for colouring

Numerals ⅞ in (22 mm), gold effect, self-adhesive plastic

Balsa cement; 3 in (75 mm) of 1/32 in (0.8 mm) brass wire; cotton thread; paints and varnish

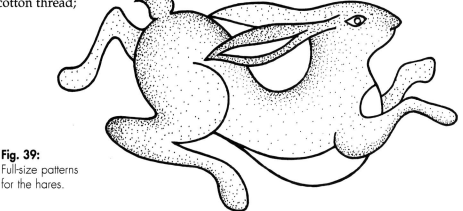

Fig. 39:
Full-size patterns for the hares.

Fig. 40:
Full-size pattern for
the rolling meadow.

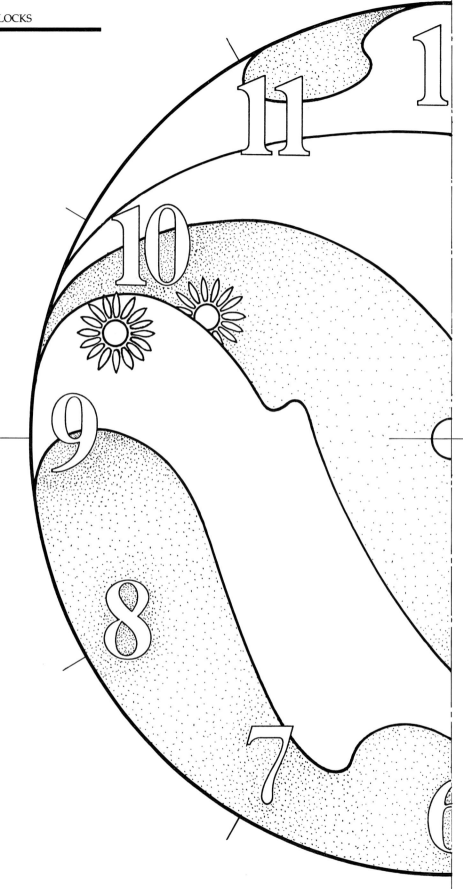

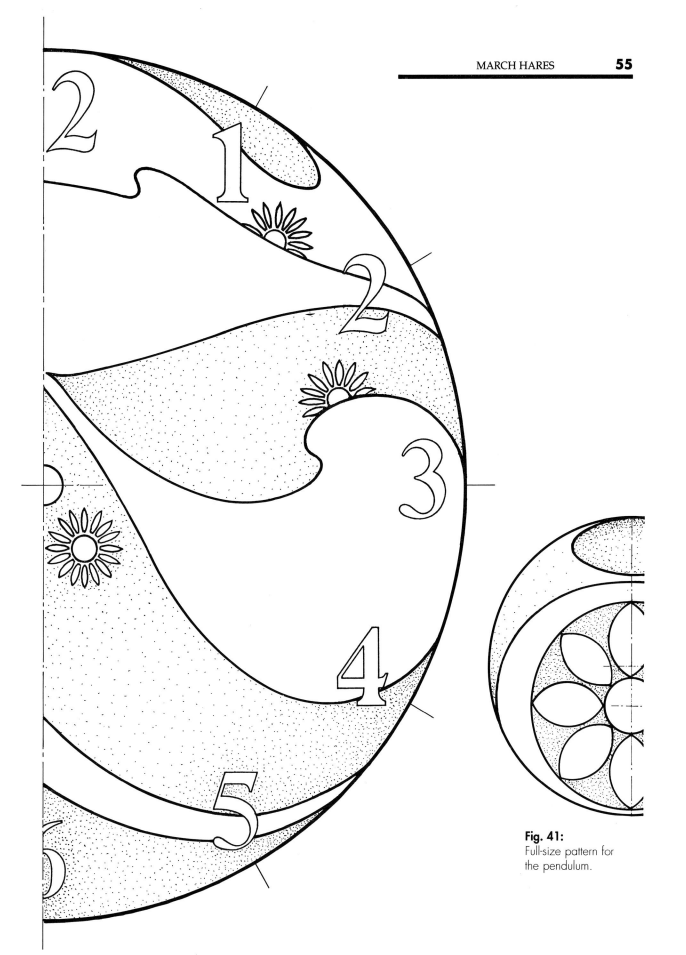

Fig. 41:
Full-size pattern for
the pendulum.

OVER THE RAINBOW

The clock is shown in the colour photograph and Fig. 44. A full-size pattern for the dial is given in Fig. 45 (page 58), for the bluebird in Fig. 46 (page 59), and for the pendulum in Fig. 47 (page 59).

Construction

The dial is built up in four layers and Fig. 42 should help with the location of part outlines on the full-size pattern. It is a good idea to cut out three, dial-sized discs, then cut the two topmost layers from one of them.

Fig. 43 (below) shows the connection between the bluebird's wire and the plastic pendulum arm. Bindings on the wire are cemented to plywood packs which are bolted to the plastic arm. Crank the wire around the wall hanger formed by cutting a 'V'-shaped notch in the strip of hardboard which links the stand-off blocks, and bend it forwards, towards the rim of the dial. The wall stand-off blocks can, of course, be deleted, and the clock hung from the plastic hanger on the movement, if the bluebird is not fitted.

A long spindle quartz movement is required for this four-layer clock to ensure that the hands clear the dial. Washers or a spacing sleeve have to be inserted beneath the tubular fixing screw, and the arrangement is described in Chapter 2.

The foreground flowers are dots of colour applied with the No. 2 brush. Compasses with a ruling pen attachment were used to edge the bands of colour on the rainbow (see Chapter 2). Colour the whole of the sky area blue before transferring the outlines of the clouds and distant hills to the first layer of the dial. If preferred, these features could be cut from thin plywood, coloured, and then stuck down, to avoid the need for careful brushwork.

Colour Scheme

Rainbow and pendulum rod purple, blue, light blue, mid green, mid yellow and bright red (use turquoise for the blue, add white for light blue)

Sky pale blue (white emulsion plus turquoise)

Clouds white

Distant hills violet (white plus purple)

Hills on second layer pale green (white plus mid green)

Hills on third layer green (mid green plus white)

Trees on third layer dark green (mid green plus ultramarine)

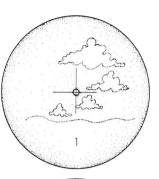

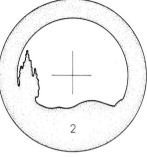

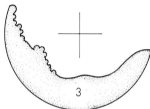

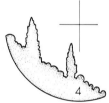

Fig. 42:
The four layers of the built-up dial.

Fig. 43:
Rear view of dial;
(a) bluebird connecting wire cranked around wall-hanger notch;
(b) hanger strip;
(c) wall stand-off blocks;
(d) hardboard packs to keep dial vertical;
(e) plywood packs bolted to plastic pendulum arm.

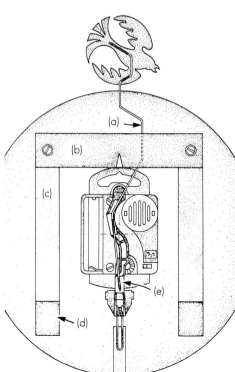

Fourth layer mid green

Path light brown (white plus brown)

Flowers orange, red, yellow and white

Pendulum bob dark green and green (mix as above)

Bluebird blue and light blue (turquoise and white plus turquoise)

Hands bright red

Optional Shading

Trees on third layer brown

Trees on fourth layer pale green (mix as above)

The dial layers are counted up from the backing disc: i.e. the clouds and distant hills are painted on to the first layer.

Materials and Parts

Bluebird and small packs on plastic pendulum arm 1/16 in (1.5 mm) plywood, 3 × 3 in (75 × 75 mm)

All other sheet parts hardboard, 24 × 21 in (610 × 535 mm)

Wall stand-off blocks two out of a 12 in (305 mm) length of softwood, 1½ × 1 in (38 × 25 mm)

Long spindle quartz movement with blind hand-fixing nut

Hands 3⅞ in (98 mm), brass for colouring

Numerals ⅞ in (22 mm), gold effect, self-adhesive plastic

Balsa cement; 12 in (305 mm) of 3/64 in (1 mm) brass wire; two small bolts for attaching plywood packs to plastic pendulum arm, 1/16 in (1.5 mm) maximum diameter × ⅜ in (10 mm) long; two ½ in (13 mm) No. 6 brass screws; washers or sleeve for movement fixing screw; cotton thread; paints and varnish

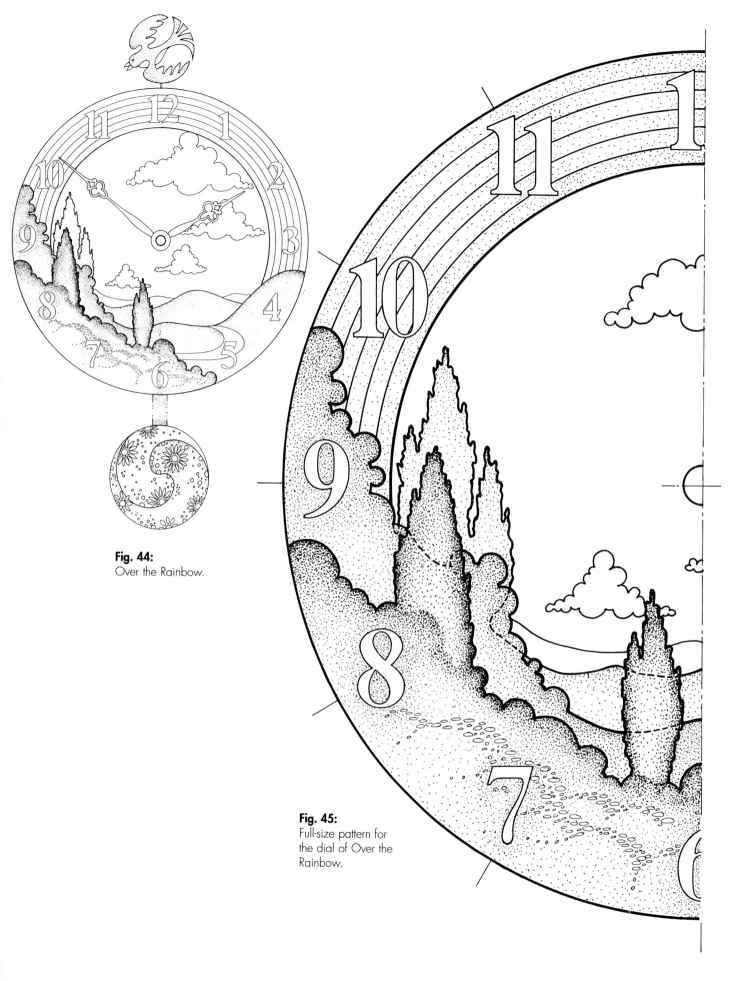

Fig. 44:
Over the Rainbow.

Fig. 45:
Full-size pattern for
the dial of Over the
Rainbow.

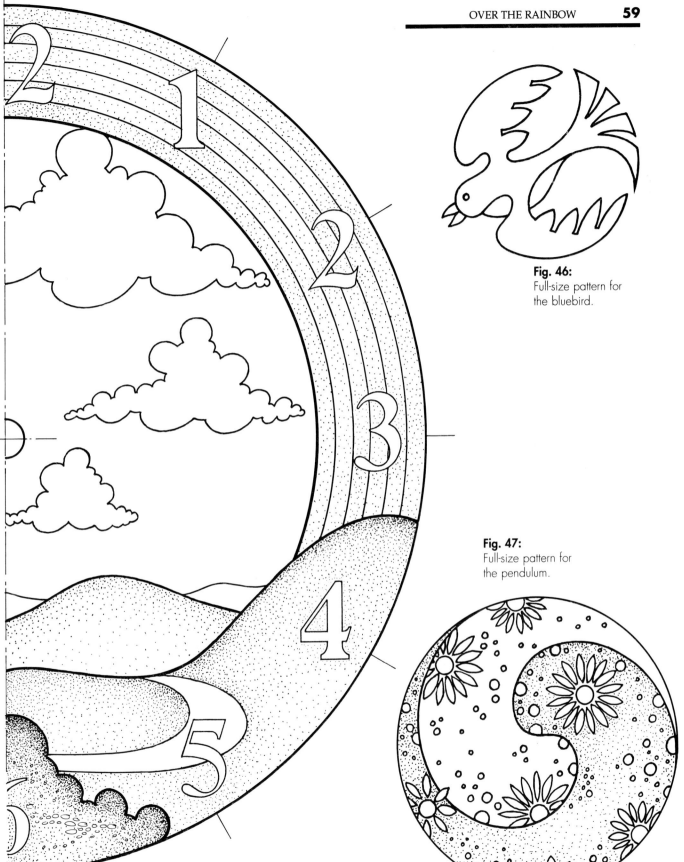

Fig. 46:
Full-size pattern for the bluebird.

Fig. 47:
Full-size pattern for the pendulum.

7 CAT CLOCKS

Deified by the ancient Egyptians and transformed into humorous icons by twentieth-century cartoonists, there is no doubt which category claims these three felines.

TOM AND JENNY

Depicted in the colour photographs on pages 64 and 65, and Figs. 48 and 51, Tom has a lean and hungry look, while Jenny's profile is softer, rounder and more feminine. Apart from this, and the very obvious differences in colouring and dial shape, the construction of the clocks is the same.

Construction

The 'exploded' view of the parts in Fig. 55 (page 63), together with Tom's back view in Fig. 56 (page 65), show how the clocks are assembled. The pendulum attachment which operates the eyes and tail is described on page 21 (see Fig. 8), and little needs to be added to the guidance given there.

Three wall stand-off blocks are cemented behind the cat. Either curve the crown of the top block, as shown, or fix it low enough to conceal it behind the head.

The plywood eyelid mount extends upwards to form the inner ears, and the whiskers are bound together with cotton thread and held in place by a groove in the nose block.

Fig. 48: Tom.

Cement hardboard packs beneath the front paws to lift them above the dial disc which is secured by the movement fixing screw.

Full-size patterns for the different body, dial and tail profiles are given in Figs. 50 (opposite), 49 (opposite), 52 (page 62) and 54 (page 63). The eye panel pattern is given in Fig. 53 (page 62).

Tom's Colour Scheme

Body and tail black

Ears pink (white plus red and a hint of black)

Eyelids violet (white plus a hint of purple)

Eye panel pale yellow (white plus mid yellow)

Eyes dark green (mid green plus blue)

Nose bright red

Whiskers, bow tie and claws mid yellow (red spots on bow tie)

Jowls, paws and tail flash white (grey spots on jowls)

Dial pale blue (white plus turquoise)

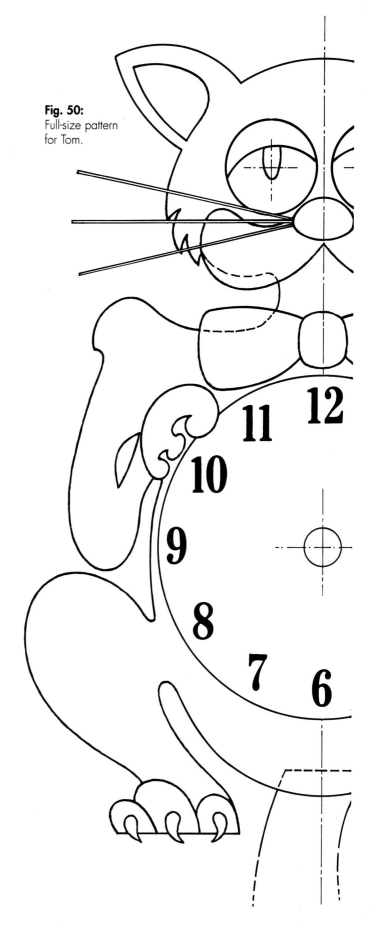

Fig. 50:
Full-size pattern for Tom.

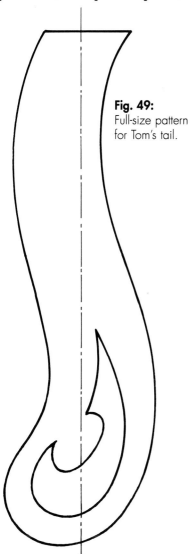

Fig. 49:
Full-size pattern for Tom's tail.

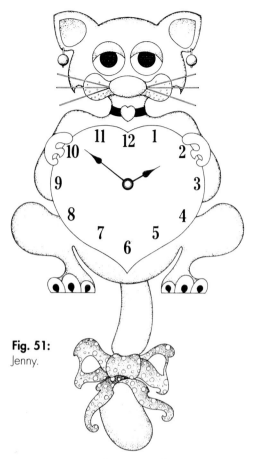

Fig. 51:
Jenny.

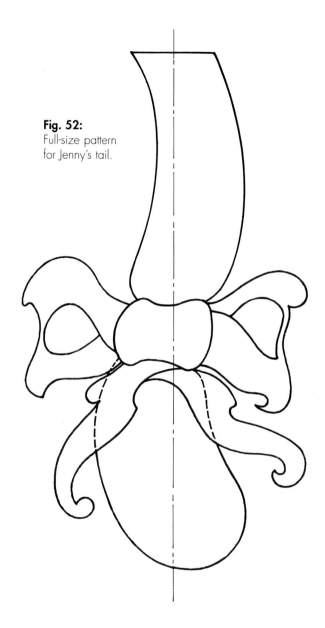

Fig. 52:
Full-size pattern
for Jenny's tail.

Jenny's Colour Scheme

Body and tail white (emulsion paint)

Ears and nose pink (white plus red with a hint of black)

Eyelids and eyes pale blue (white plus turquoise)

Eye pupils blue (turquoise)

Eye panel very pale blue (white plus a hint of turquoise)

Jowls and paws grey (white plus black, white spots on jowls)

Earrings, locket, dial and claws bright red

Choker (neck band) black

Bow on tail mid blue (ultramarine plus turquoise)

Optional shading on bow and ribbons blue (turquoise)

Fig. 53:
Full-size pattern
for Tom's eye panel.

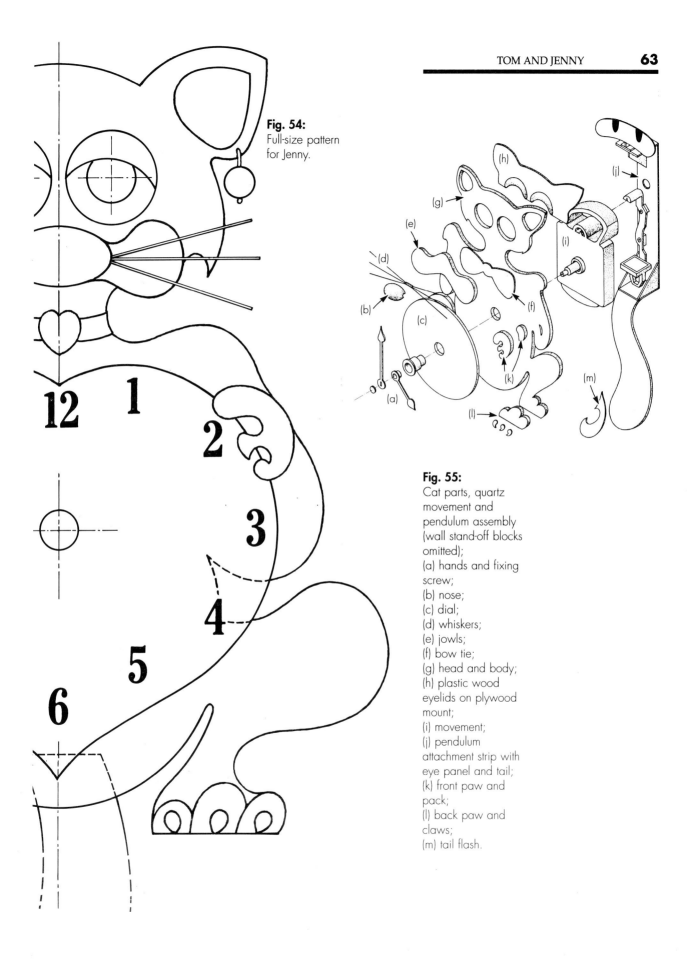

Fig. 54:
Full-size pattern
for Jenny.

12 1

2

3

4

5

6

Fig. 55:
Cat parts, quartz
movement and
pendulum assembly
(wall stand-off blocks
omitted);
(a) hands and fixing
screw;
(b) nose;
(c) dial;
(d) whiskers;
(e) jowls;
(f) bow tie;
(g) head and body;
(h) plastic wood
eyelids on plywood
mount;
(i) movement;
(j) pendulum
attachment strip with
eye panel and tail;
(k) front paw and
pack;
(l) back paw and
claws;
(m) tail flash.

Materials and Parts

The following items will construct *one* cat:

Body, tail, jowls, paws and dial hardboard, 12 × 12 in (305 × 305 mm)

Pendulum attachment strip, packs, platforms and gussets; eye panel, eye panel bracket and bow tie or tail bow 1/16 in (1.5 mm) thick plywood, 6 × 6 in (150 × 150 mm)

Eyelid mount, claws and flash on tail or locket 1/32 in (0.8 mm) or 1/64 in (0.4 mm) plywood, 6 × 2 in (150 × 50 mm)

Eyelids plastic wood

Nose softwood block, 1⅜ × 1 × ½ in (35 × 25 × 13 mm), or form from plastic wood

Wall stand-off blocks three out of 9 in (230 mm) length of softwood, 1½ × ¾ in (38 × 19 mm)

Medium spindle quartz movement an open hand-fixing nut will be required if a second hand is fitted

Hands 1⅝ in (41 mm) black finish

Second hand (if required) 1¼ in (30 mm) red or black finish to contrast with dial colour

Numerals ⅜ in (10 mm), black, rub-down transfer

Balsa cement; 18 in (460 mm) of 1/32 in (0.8 mm) brass wire; brass picture hanger with two small self-tapping screws; small self-tapping screw for eye panel bracket (not required if bracket is cemented into position); two small bolts for pendulum attachment, 1/16 in (1.5 mm) maximum diameter × ⅜ in (10 mm) long, complete with nuts; cotton thread; self-adhesive paper label for eyes; beads (for Jenny's earrings); paints and varnish.

Jenny

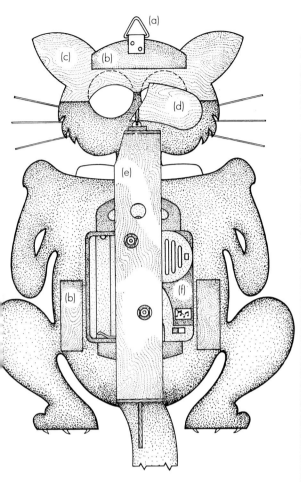

Fig. 56:
Rear view of Tom;
(a) picture hanger;
(b) wall stand-off
blocks;
(c) eyelid mount;
(d) eye panel cut
away to reveal eye
sockets;
(e) pendulum
attachment strip;
(f) movement.

Tom

THE MAD MOUSER

This clock, illustrated in both the colour photograph on page 68 and Fig. 57, is the most complicated in the collection. The tail wags while the eyes, tongue and paw follow the grinning mouse in an endlessly frustrating cycle of chase and escape. The clock can be displayed on a table or mantelpiece, or hung from the wall.

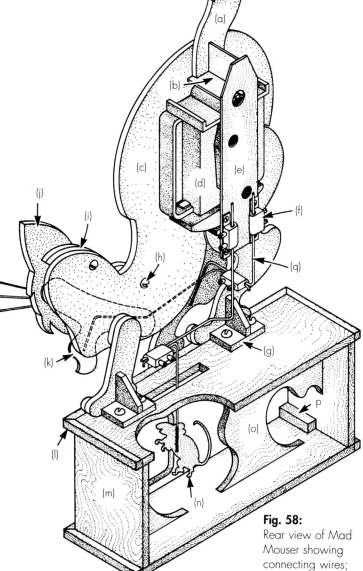

Fig. 57:
The Mad Mouser.

Fig. 58:
Rear view of Mad Mouser showing connecting wires;
(a) tail;
(b) top platform and gusset;
(c) cat's body;
(d) movement;
(e) pendulum attachment strip;
(f) terminals fixed to strip;
(g) fixing brackets;
(h) screws securing face piece;
(i) head pack;
(j) face piece;
(k) 'T'-shaped eye and tongue piece;
(l) beading;
(m) plinth;
(n) mouse;
(o) screen;
(p) fillets positioning screen;
(q) connecting wires.

Construction

The rear view of the clock, given in Fig. 58, shows how the pendulum drive is linked to the moving parts. The plastic hanger has to be removed from the case of the quartz unit so that the connection between tail and pendulum attachment strip can be low enough to be concealed behind the cat's body.

The wires which support and operate the moving parts are fixed to the bottom end of the plywood strip by means of electrical connectors cut from a 5-amp terminal block (the type with a row of terminals embedded in polythene). This eases the task of adjusting the position of

Fig. 59:
Full-size pattern for body, legs, head pack, and eye and tongue panel.

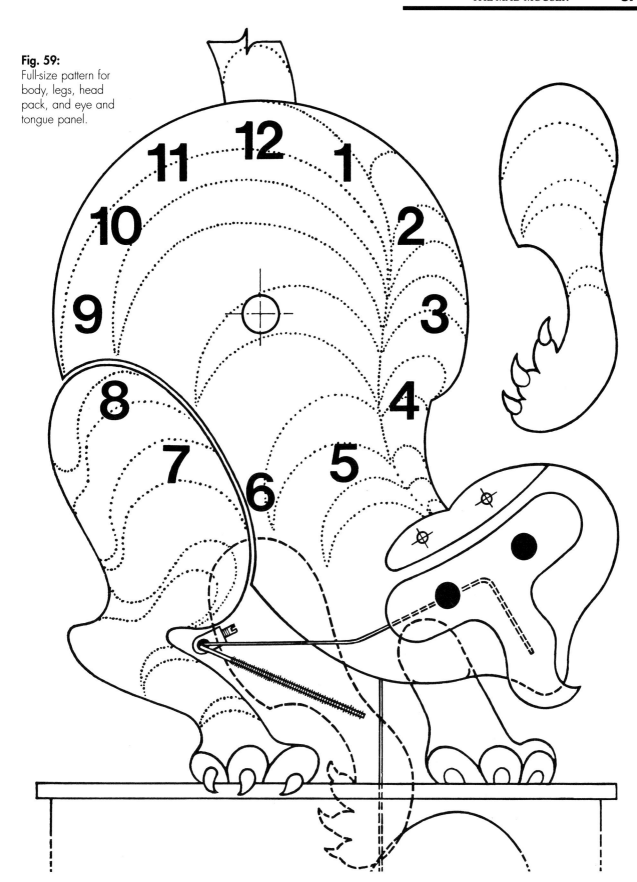

The Mad Mouser

moving parts after the initial assembly. The connectors are soldered to strips of brass, the strips being drilled for fixing to the plywood pendulum attachment by small, self-tapping screws.

Constructors who wish to avoid soldering could cement the terminals in place with cyanoacrylate or two-part epoxy resin adhesive. If adhesive is used, abrade the metal and de-grease it with methylated spirits (methyl alchohol in the USA) or the bond may be poor.

The 'T'-shaped eye and tongue panel shares a wire connector with the moving paw. The two-layer hardboard pack which spaces the face from the body creates a ¼ in (6 mm) slot for the eye and tongue piece, and setting up is not too critical. Cement the hardboard spacers to the back of the face and secure the face assembly to the body by means of two small, self-tapping screws. The ability to remove the face assembly and expose the eyes and tongue is of help during the setting up and adjustment process.

Use ¹⁄₁₆ in (1.5 mm) diameter wire for the connection to the paw and for the link between the plywood pendulum strip and the terminal above the mouse slot. Use ¹⁄₃₂ in (0.8 mm) wire for the connection to the eye and tongue piece and for the drop to the mouse.

The rear leg is cut separately from the body to define the form of the cat more clearly and to ease the colouring process. A hardboard plate links the leg to the body and extends behind the movement to increase the dial thickness to ¼ in (6 mm). The outline of this plate is not critical and it has not been shown on the figures in the interests of clarity. Cement hardboard brackets to the feet and secure these to the plinth with self-tapping screws.

The method of assembling the eyelids, ears, nose, whiskers and jowls is the same as for Tom and Jenny (see Fig. 55, page 63). Full-size patterns for the body, legs, head pack, and the eye and tongue piece, are given in Fig. 59 (page 67).

Patterns for the face, tail, mouse, mouse hole and plinth are included in Fig. 60.

The 2 in (50 mm) deep plinth is constructed from ³⁄₁₆ in (5 mm) thick plywood. An internal plywood screen, held off the front face by ¾ in (19 mm) long fillets, is painted matt black to form

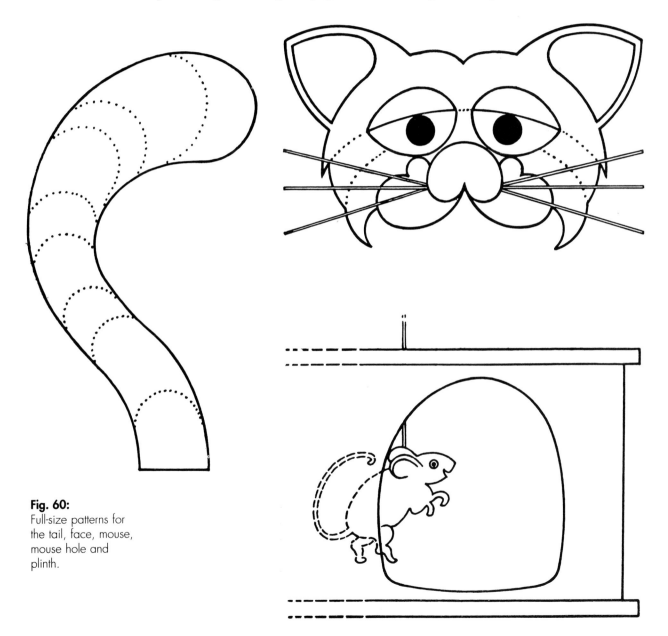

Fig. 60:
Full-size patterns for the tail, face, mouse, mouse hole and plinth.

a background against which the moving mouse can be clearly seen.

Use a try square or set square when marking out and assembling the plinth parts to ensure right-angled corners. Scribe the setting-out lines with a Stanley knife. This will limit splintering when the parts are cut out with the saw.

A beading is applied to mask the edges of the plywood and add interest to the plinth. This should, preferably, be mitred at the corners.

Colour Scheme

Body pale orange (white plus orange)

Stripes deep orange (orange plus red)

Inner ears very pale orange (white plus body colour)

Eyelids blue (turquoise plus white)

Eye pupils black

Eye panel, jowls, fixed paws and mouse white (yellow spots on jowls, white spots on moving paw)

Nose, tongue and claws red

Whiskers brass

Plinth faint yellowish-brown tint (stain plywood with a *very* watery mix of yellow and brown poster colour, or use thinned oak wood stain)

Screen inside plinth black (use poster colour or black ink)

Materials and Parts

Cat body, legs, tail, paws, face, jowls, face and leg packs; back leg fixing plate, and brackets for fixing cat to plinth hardboard, 12 × 9 in (305 × 230 mm)

Pendulum attachment strip, packs, platform and gussets; and mouse 1/16 in (1.5 mm) thick plywood, 6 × 3 in (150 × 75 mm)

Eyelid mount and inner ears, eye and tongue 'T'-piece and claws 1/32 in (0.8 mm) thick plywood, 4 × 4 in (100 × 100 mm)

Eyelids plastic wood

Nose softwood block, 1 × 3/4 × 1/2 in (25 × 19 × 13 mm), or form from plastic wood

Plinth top, bottom, sides and screen 3/16 in (5 mm) thick plywood, 12 × 12 in (305 × 305 mm)

Plinth trim and fillets which position the screen 30 in (760 mm) of 1/4 × 1/4 in (6 × 6 mm) softwood strip

Medium spindle quartz movement with open hand-fixing nut

Hands 1 7/8 in (49 mm), black finish

Second hand 1 1/4 in (30 mm), black finish

Numerals 3/8 in (10 mm), black, rub-down transfer

Balsa cement; 12 in (305 mm) of 1/16 in (1.5 mm) diameter brass wire; 24 in (610 mm) of 1/32 in (0.8 mm) brass wire; two small bolts for pendulum attachment strip, 1/16 in (1.5 mm) maximum diameter × 3/8 in (10 mm) long, complete with nuts; four 5-amp terminals (cut from a polythene connector block); ten small self-tapping screws, 1/16 in (1.5 mm) diameter × 1/4 in (6 mm) long, for assembling the cat's head, attaching the cat to the plinth, and fixing the terminals to the plywood pendulum strip; 2 in (50 mm) of 1/4 × 1/32 in (6 × 0.8 mm) brass strip; flux-cored solder and soldering iron; self-adhesive paper label (for the eyes); cotton thread; paints and varnish.

If adhesive is used to secure the terminals to the plywood pendulum attachment, four of the self-tapping screws, the brass strip, solder and soldering iron will not be required.

8 CREATURES OF THE SEA

The sea is the common element which links these three, very different clocks.

Fig. 61:
Penguins.

PENGUINS

Crimson sun and hands inject a note of warmth into this clock depicted in both the colour photograph (page 73) and Fig. 61, where Antarctic wastes of sea and snow form a chilly back-drop to the flock of penguins drifting along on an ice floe.

Construction

The dial is built up in four layers, and Fig. 62 (page 72) should be of help in identifying the part outlines in the full-size pattern given in Fig. 64 (page 75). The penguins are cut from 1/16 in (1.5 mm) thick plywood and cemented into place after colouring. The young penguins adjacent to the seven on the dial are cemented down on top of the larger parent birds. If preferred, the sun and distant iceberg can be cut from 1/32 in (0.8 mm) or 1/64 in (0.4 mm) thick plywood and coloured before being stuck in place.

The sea steps forward on to successive layers of the dial, and a ruling pen will be found useful for defining the horizon and the iceberg waterlines. The pale blue tones on the ice are applied with the No. 6 brush.

With four layers of hardboard plus the penguins, even a long- spindle quartz movement will not elevate the hands above the perimeter of the dial, so they have to be bent slightly, at the pivot, to give the necessary clearance. Washers or a spacing sleeve are required for the tubular screw which fixes the movement, and these arrangements are described and illustrated in Chapter 2.

The simple design on the optional pendulum bob harmonizes with the dial, and a full-size pattern is given in Fig. 63 (page 74). If preferred, the design can be cut out with the fretsaw and cemented to a backing disc after colouring. This bob is suspended on a brass rod which is hooked over the plastic arm on the quartz movement. Bind the lower end of the rod with thread and cement it to the hardboard bob.

Colour Scheme

Sun and hands bright red

Sea blue (turquoise)

Penguin backs and wings black

Beaks and flippers orange

Use emulsion paint for the white areas, and tint white emulsion with various amounts of turquoise to produce the different shades of blue for the sky and ice. With the colour photograph as a guide, it will not be difficult to create the desired effect.

Materials and Parts

Penguins 1/16 in (1.5 mm) thick plywood, 6 × 4 in (150 × 100 mm)

Sun and distant iceberg (if stuck on) 1/32 in (0.8 mm) or 1/64 in (0.4 mm) thick plywood, 2½ × 2½ in (65 × 65 mm)

All other sheet parts for dial and pendulum bob hardboard, 24 × 21 in (610 × 535 mm)

Long spindle quartz movement with blind hand-fixing nut

Hands 3⅞ in (98 mm), brass for colouring

Balsa cement; 9 in (230 mm) of 3/16 × 1/32 in (5 × 0.8 mm) brass strip for pendulum rod; washers or sleeve for movement fixing screw; cotton thread; paints and varnish

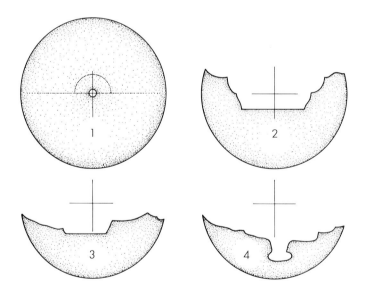

Fig. 62:
The four layers of the built-up dial.

Fig. 63:
Full-size pattern for
the pendulum.

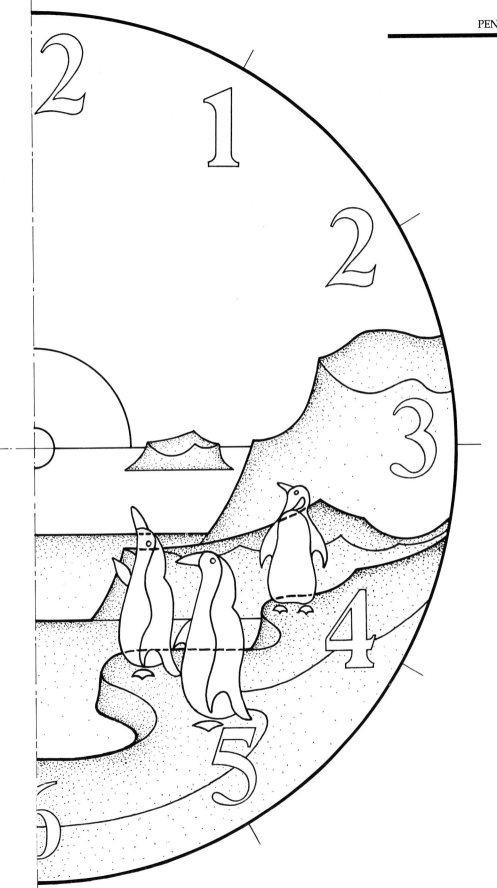

Fig. 64:
Full-size pattern for the
Penguins dial.

PISCES

The gliding fish design shown in both the colour photograph and Fig. 65 (page 78) has obvious astrological associations. Vivid colours make it very eye-catching.

Construction

A full-size pattern for the dial is given in Fig. 66 (page 78), and for the optional pendulum in Fig. 67 (page 79). The fish bodies and tails are cut from hardboard; and the fins, gills, eyes and all but the smallest of the bubbles are cut from ¹⁄₁₆ in (1.5 mm) thick plywood.

The swirling water design on the dial, and the boundary between the two tones of yellow on the bodies of the fish, were defined with the No. 6 brush. If preferred (and it would probably take no more time), the dial pattern can be cut out with the fretsaw and assembled on a backing disc of hardboard after colouring. Similarly, the colour boundary along the fish bodies can be cut and the separate parts coloured before being cemented to the dial.

Hands and self-adhesive numerals were primed and painted. If preferred, the brass and gold finishes can be left exposed. They add glitter to the dial, but the colouring gives greater contrast and legibility.

Colour Scheme

Swirling water ultramarine and turquoise

Fish bodies mid yellow and pale yellow (white plus mid yellow)

Gills orange

Top fin pale yellow (mix as above)

Head bright red

Eye and bubbles pale blue (white plus turquoise)

Eye pupil turquoise

Hands, numerals and pendulum rod pale yellow (mix as above)

Optional shading

Bubbles white (tadpole-shaped highlight)

Hands, numerals and pendulum rod mid yellow and orange

Materials and Parts

Dial, fish bodies and tails, pendulum rod and bob hardboard, 18 × 12 in (460 × 305 mm), or 21 × 15 in (535 × 380 mm), if a backing disc is used

Gills, fins, eyes and bubbles ¹⁄₁₆ in (1.5 mm) thick plywood, 6 × 6 in (150 × 150 mm)

Medium spindle quartz movement with blind hand-fixing nut

Hands 3⅞ in (98 mm), brass for colouring

Numerals ⅞ in (22 mm), gold finish, self-adhesive plastic

Balsa cement; 3 in (75 mm) length of ¹⁄₃₂ in (0.8 mm) diameter brass wire; cotton thread; paints and varnish

Fig. 65:
Pisces.

Fig. 66:
Full-size pattern for
the dial of Pisces.

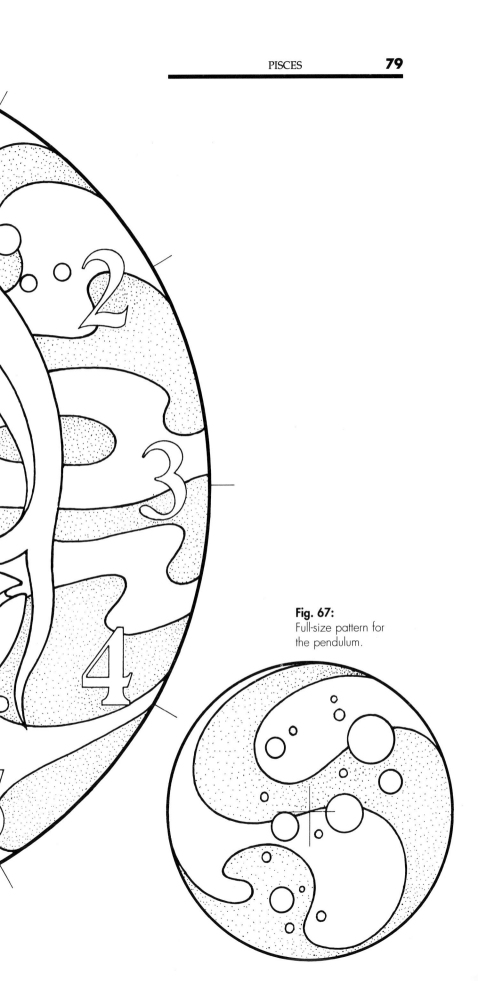

Fig. 67:
Full-size pattern for the pendulum.

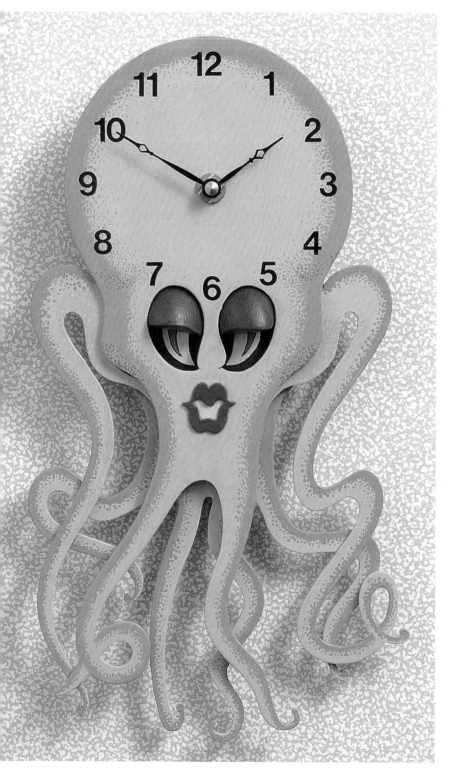

OCTAVIA OCTOPUS

This clock is shown in both the colour photograph and Fig. 69 (page 82). Writhing legs and roving eyes bring the design to life, while the huge eyelids echo the shape and form of the head. Together with the mouth, they give the dial a distinctly feminine appearance. Real octopuses have beak-like mouth parts, but a feature of this kind would make the clock appear sinister in a way that could frighten a small child, so the human mouth was substituted.

Construction

The clock comprises the head and four fixed legs, together with four moving legs which are powered by the pendulum drive unit. Fig. 70 (page 82) should help with the identification of the various parts in the full-size pattern in Fig. 68 (opposite). The two outer, fixed legs are separate pieces, secured by lugs cemented behind the face. This layering is not essential, but it does enhance the three-dimensional effect.

Fig. 71 (page 82) depicts the method of attaching the swinging eye and leg piece to the pendulum arm on the movement. Slots in the hardboard enable it to fit snugly around the webs on the rear face of the plastic arm. The tiny rectangle of 1/16 in (1.5 mm) plywood is located on the dial side of the arm, and a small self-tapping screw is passed through the plywood and the aperture in the arm, and driven into the hardboard part to lock it in position. The leg and eye piece must be fixed rigidly to the plastic arm and parallel to the back of the head. If it is able to twist, it will bind on the back

Fig. 68:
Full-size pattern for the face and legs. The radius of the dial is 2½ in (63 mm).

1¼ in (32 mm)

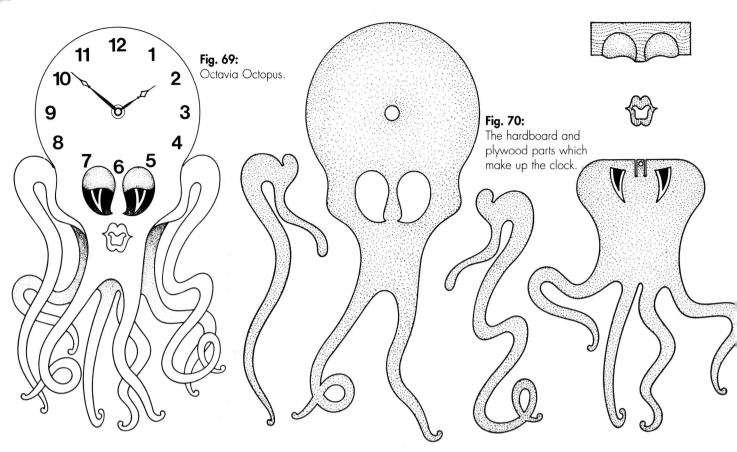

Fig. 69:
Octavia Octopus.

Fig. 70:
The hardboard and plywood parts which make up the clock.

of the head and stop the pendulum action.

Although not essential, a separate card or plywood eye panel, packed off the moving legs part, will bring the eyes closer to the face and make their movement more noticeable. The plastic wood eyelids should project at least ⅜ in (10 mm) beyond the face of the dial.

Colour Scheme

Body and legs lime green (white plus yellow plus mid green)

Eyelids purple

Eye panel deep blue (ultramarine plus a hint of black)

Eyes mid yellow

Eye pupils deep lime green (mix as body colour but add less white)

Lips bright red

Optional shading to head and legs deep lime green (mix as above)

Materials and Parts

Body and legs hardboard, 15 × 12 in (380 × 305 mm)

Eyelid mount 1⁄32 in (0.8 mm) thick plywood, 3 × 1½ in (75 × 38 mm)

Eyelids plastic wood

Mouth and plate for pendulum attachment 1⁄16 in (1.5 mm) thick plywood, 2 × 1 in (50 × 25 mm)

Short spindle quartz movement and blind hand-fixing nut (or use a medium spindle unit and fit a hardboard washer behind the dial)

Hands 1⅞ in (49 mm), black finish

Numerals ⅜ in (10 mm), black, rub-down transfer

Balsa cement; self-adhesive paper label (for eyes); self-tapping screw, 1⁄16 in (1.5 mm) diameter × ¼ in (6 mm) long; paints and varnish

Fig. 71:
Method of fixing swinging eye and leg piece to the pendulum arm on the movement (see page 80).

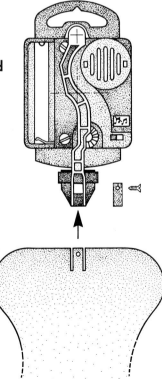

9 CROAKER AND CLUCKER

Frog and fowl are transformed by fashion and culture into the absurd extravaganzas which form the dials of these two whimsical clocks.

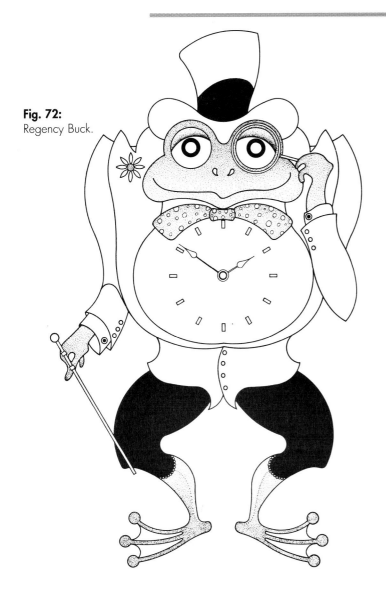

Fig. 72: Regency Buck.

REGENCY BUCK

Any princess will tell you that the old frog-kissing routine becomes quite a bore. Maybe if she'd met this dashing young buck she wouldn't have felt quite so bad about it. With his wagging legs, flashing eyes, and impeccable dress sense, this prince-for-a-kiss is depicted in both the colour photograph on page 85 and Fig. 72.

Construction

Full-size patterns are given in Figs. 74 (page 86), 75 (page 87), 76 (page 88) and 77 (page 88). Fig. 74 shows how the head, eyelids and top hat are assembled, and Fig. 75 gives the profiles for the body piece and the jacket lapels, which are cut as a separate item. The rear view, Fig. 73 (page 84), shows the pendulum attachment, eye panel, legs, and the three wall stand-off blocks.

Small hardboard packs are located beneath the forearms at the elbows. The two-layer pack on the monocle side has to be carved and abraded into a wedge shape to tilt the arm forwards and lift the monocle clear of the face.

Make sure the hardboard is well supported and work carefully when cutting out the feet, as they are fragile until the plywood webs are cemented in position.

A toy magnifying glass (of the kind found in Christmas crackers) will serve as the monocle. Failing this, a suitable item can be constructed from a disc of acetate or a small lens. Form the frame

from a loop of brass wire with the ends twisted together and slid inside a short length of brass tubing to form the handle.

The swagger stick can be a length of brass tubing with a bead or decorated pin as the head. Bind the monocle handle and the stick with thread and cement them to the frog's 'hands'.

The hat band, nostrils, mouth, cuffs, buttons and the decorations to the legs of the breeches, are painted with the No. 2 brush. The flower is painted on to a plywood disc and then stuck down on the lapel of the jacket.

The crown of the hat must be securely cemented to the head because this joint carries the full weight of the clock. The hat brim is, of course, mounted on top of the face piece.

Colour Scheme

Hat and jacket lapels deep pink (white plus red)

Jacket, spots on bow tie, monocle rim and decorations on legs of breeches pink (white plus red)

Breeches and bow tie purple

Face, hands, shins and flippers mid green

Flipper webs and calves pale green (white plus mid green)

Shirt front, cuffs and eye panel white (emulsion paint)

Eyes black

Eye pupils orange

Mouth bright red

Nostrils brown

Fig. 73:
Rear view; (a) picture hanger fixed to wall stand-off block; (b) plywood eyelid mount; (c) eye panel cut away to expose sockets; (d) plywood pendulum attachment strip; (e) movement; (f) wall stand-off blocks; (g) gussets to stiffen connection to wagging legs; (h) plywood feet webs.

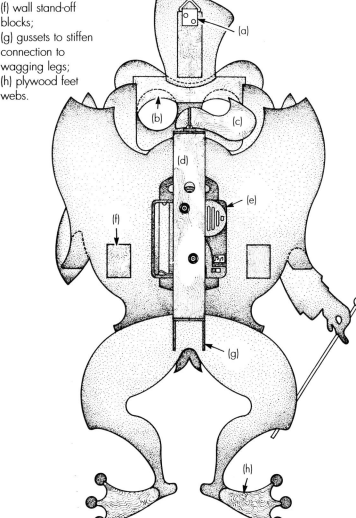

Regency Buck

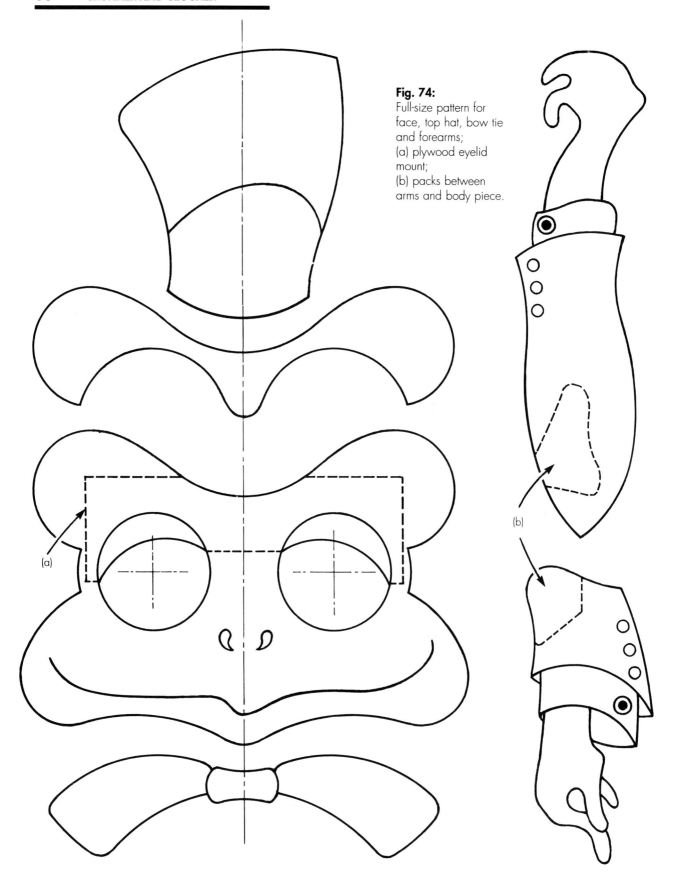

Fig. 74:
Full-size pattern for face, top hat, bow tie and forearms;
(a) plywood eyelid mount;
(b) packs between arms and body piece.

(a)

(b)

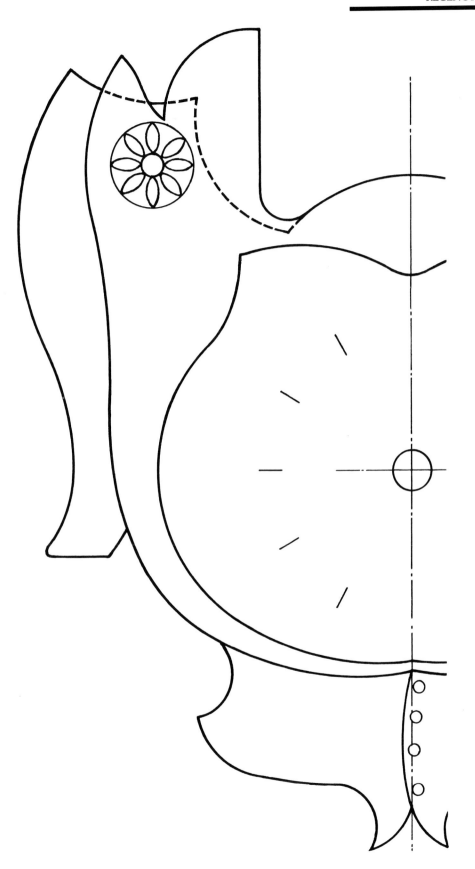

Fig. 75:
Full-size pattern for
jacket and jacket
lapels.

Materials and Parts

Pendulum attachment strips, packs, platforms and gussets; and eye panel $\frac{1}{16}$ in (1.5 mm) thick plywood, 6×4 in (150×100 mm)

Eyelid mount, bow tie and flipper webs $\frac{1}{32}$ in (0.8 mm) or $\frac{1}{64}$ in (0.4 mm) thick plywood, 5×3 in (125×75 mm)

All other sheet parts hardboard, 18×15 in (460×380 mm)

Eyelids plastic wood

Wall stand-off blocks three out of a 6 in (150 mm) length of softwood, $1\frac{1}{2} \times \frac{3}{4}$ in (38×19 mm)

Short spindle quartz movement with blind hand-fixing nut (or use a medium spindle unit and insert a hardboard washer behind the dial)

Hands $1\frac{5}{8}$ in (41 mm), brass finish

Markers $\frac{1}{4}$ in (6 mm), gold finish, self-adhesive plastic

Balsa cement; 7 in (180 mm) of $\frac{3}{32}$ in (2.5 mm) brass tube; 7 in (180 mm) of $\frac{1}{32}$ in (0.8 mm) brass wire and small piece of acetate for monocle (or use a toy magnifying glass); bead or decorated pin for head of swagger stick; cotton thread; picture hanger with two small self-tapping screws; small self-tapping screw for eye panel bracket (not required if bracket cemented in position); two small bolts for pendulum attachment, $\frac{1}{16}$ in (1.5 mm) maximum diameter $\times \frac{3}{8}$ in (10 mm) long, complete with nuts; self-adhesive paper label (for eyes); paints and varnish

Warning to Lady Woodworkers

Lady woodworkers who are also princesses are warned that if they kiss the completed clock they will get a life-size hardboard prince powered by a quartz movement.

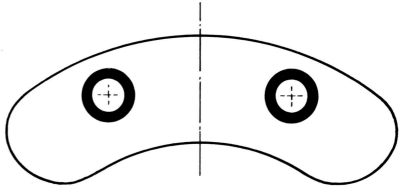

Fig. 76: Full-size pattern for eye panel.

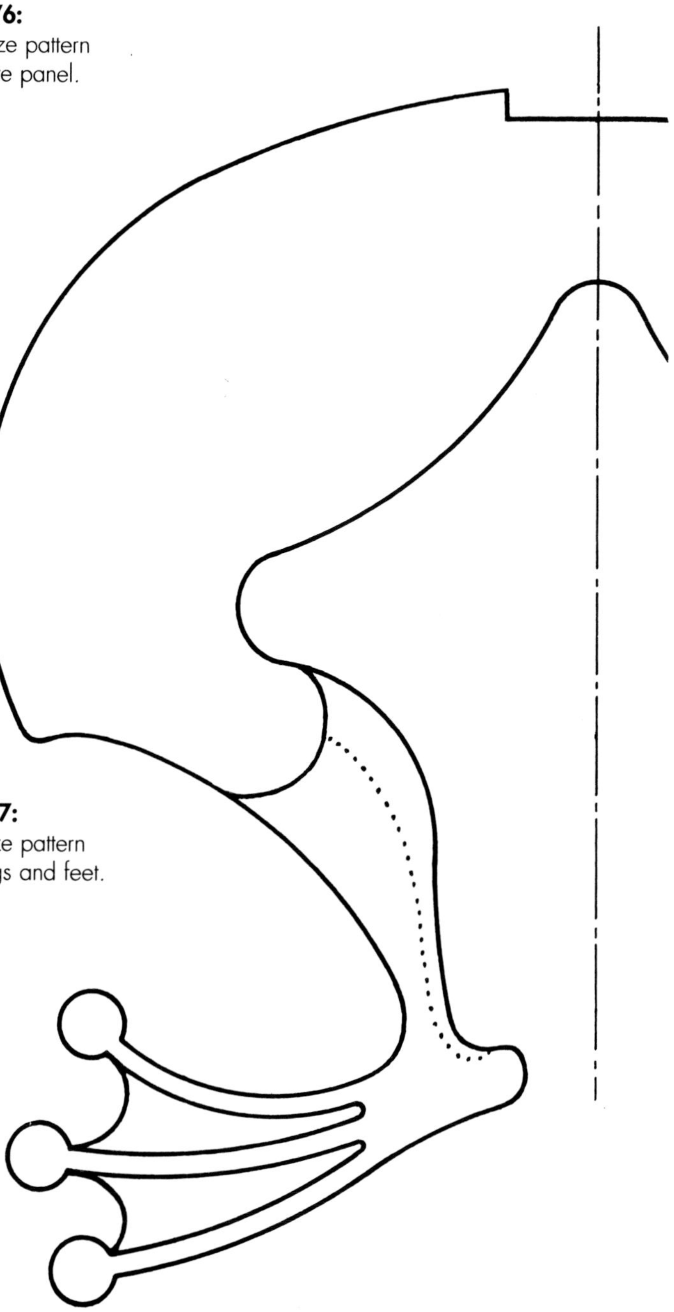

Fig. 77: Full-size pattern for legs and feet.

CHUKALOO TUTU

Illustrated in both the colour photograph (page 92) and Fig. 78, this rooster has all the hauteur of a great prima donna. She wiggles her tutu and flutters a wing while pirouetting on her blue ballet shoes.

Full-size patterns for the various parts are given in Figs. 81, 82 and 83 (page 91). The rear view, Fig. 79, shows the pendulum attachment and the wing balancing system, and this is further clarified by the side view in Fig. 80 (page 90).

Construction

The dress is a separate top layer, cemented to the body after colouring. The area of the comb which droops to the left is part of the body sheet. Cut a ⅜ in (10 mm) diameter bead in half for the eyes, and form the beak from plastic wood.

The plastic wall hanger has to be removed from the movement case to make room for the wing spacer block. Three or four small coins or washers taped to a plywood strip counterbalance the wing. Adjust the number of coins, and their position along the strip, until the legs are vertical when at rest. The counterbalance strip is cemented to the

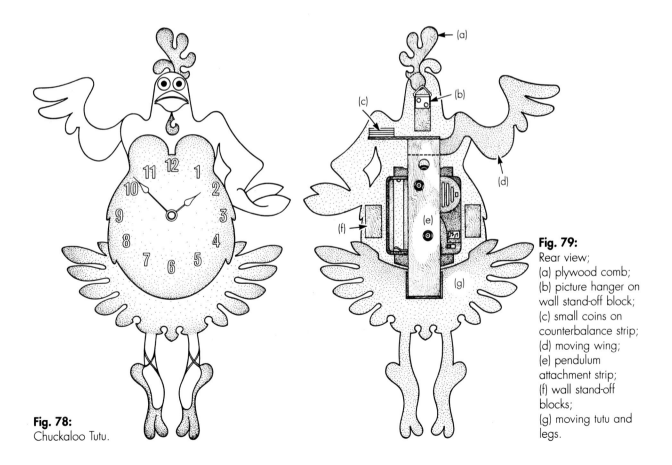

Fig. 78:
Chuckaloo Tutu.

Fig. 79:
Rear view;
(a) plywood comb;
(b) picture hanger on wall stand-off block;
(c) small coins on counterbalance strip;
(d) moving wing;
(e) pendulum attachment strip;
(f) wall stand-off blocks;
(g) moving tutu and legs.

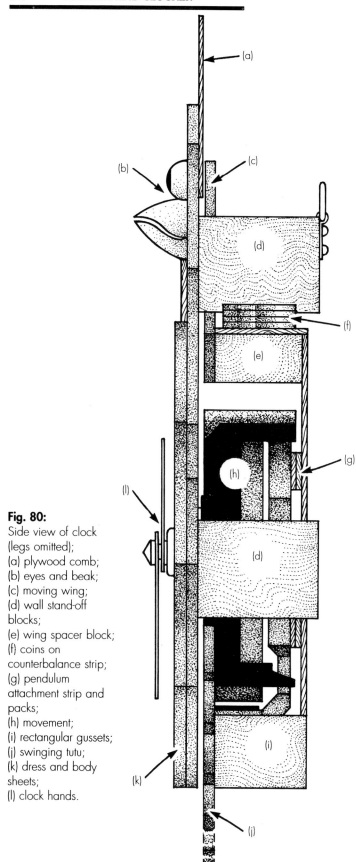

Fig. 80:
Side view of clock
(legs omitted);
(a) plywood comb;
(b) eyes and beak;
(c) moving wing;
(d) wall stand-off
blocks;
(e) wing spacer block;
(f) coins on
counterbalance strip;
(g) pendulum
attachment strip and
packs;
(h) movement;
(i) rectangular gussets;
(j) swinging tutu;
(k) dress and body
sheets;
(l) clock hands.

top of the block which attaches the wing
to the plywood pendulum extension.

With the movement fixed temporarily,
measure the distance between the
plywood pendulum extension and the
back of the dial. Deduct the thickness of
the wing plus a small amount for
clearance, and cut the wing attachment
block to this dimension.

Numerals

Gold-effect, rub-down transfer numerals
are to be preferred for this design: black
numerals would be too overpowering. If
these prove difficult to obtain, substitute
¼ in (6 mm), gold-finish, self-adhesive
plastic markers.

Colour Scheme

Body, wings, tail and legs white
(emulsion paint)

Comb and crop bright red

Beak deep orange (orange plus red)

Eyes mid yellow

Eye pupils black

Dress and ballet shoes blue (turquoise)

Optional Shading

(Colour dress white if shading technique
adopted)

'Arms' and 'shoulders' pale blue (white
plus turquoise)

Dress mid blue (ultramarine plus
turquoise), blue (turquoise), pale blue
(mix as above)

Tutu (or tail) blue (turquoise), pale blue
(mix as above)

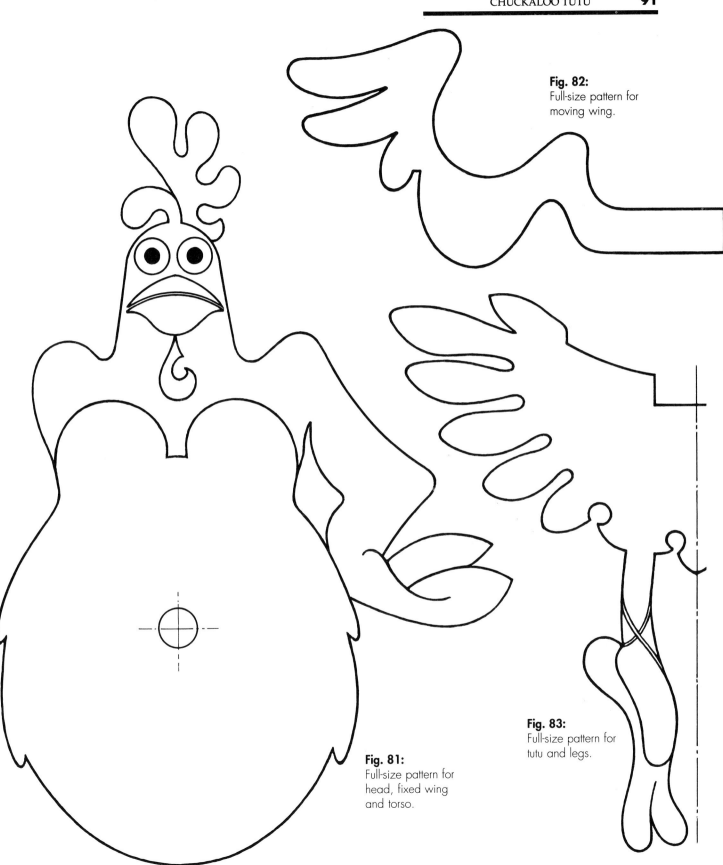

Fig. 82: Full-size pattern for moving wing.

Fig. 81: Full-size pattern for head, fixed wing and torso.

Fig. 83: Full-size pattern for tutu and legs.

Chuckaloo Tutu

Materials and Parts

Wings, body, dress, tutu and legs hardboard, 18 × 9 in (460 × 230 mm)

Pendulum attachment strip, packs, platform, and gussets; counterbalance strip, mount for beak, and the comb and crop ¹⁄₁₆ in (1.5 mm) thick plywood, 6 × 3 in (150 × 75 mm)

Wall stand-off blocks and wing spacer block all out of a 6 in (150 mm) length of softwood, 1½ × ¾ in (38 × 19 mm)

Medium spindle quartz movement with blind hand-fixing nut

Hands 1⅝ in (41 mm) brass finish

Numerals ⅜ in (10 mm) gold effect rub-down transfers, or ¼ in (6 mm) gold-finish, self-adhesive plastic markers

Balsa cement; ⅜ in (10 mm) diameter bead; brass picture hanger with two self-tapping screws; two small bolts for pendulum attachment, ¹⁄₁₆ in (1.5 mm) maximum diameter × ⅜ in (10 mm) long, complete with two nuts; small coins or washers; paints and varnish

10 THE AGE OF STEAM

This chapter is devoted to the construction of two clocks which celebrate the culmination of the age of steam.

OCEAN LINER

Illustrated in the colour photograph (page 96) and in Figs. 84 (below), 85 (page 94), and 86 (page 95), the sun rays and stylized liner capture the Art Deco flavour of the 1920s and 1930s when many of these huge ships were built.

Construction

The clock is built up in four layers, as shown in Fig. 86, and apertures are cut in the first three to form a chamber for a short spindle quartz movement. If a medium spindle unit is fitted, leave the two top layers intact to ensure sufficient panel thickness.

Sun, sun rays and palm trees are painted on to the circular backing disc, and the distant island, clouds, smoke and liner are then cemented in position after colouring. If preferred, the sun and the sun rays can be cut out with the fretsaw and assembled on a backing disc after they have been coloured.

The hard edges of colour on the funnel of the liner were formed with the No. 2 brush. The colour boundaries on the hull and the red and black line which defines the bow were drawn in with a ruling pen using a French curve as a guide. Again, constructors who prefer to minimize the need for careful brushwork can cut the white hull areas and red waterline from thin plywood and stick them down after colouring.

The baton hands, red second hand and plain hour markers complement the dial's Art Deco overtones. If a pendulum is required, a 3 in (75 mm) diameter bob, coloured the same vivid blue as the sea and suspended on a bright red rod, would be suitable. The pendulum-driving quartz movement would have to be a long-spindle type with the case fully exposed behind the dial.

Colour Scheme

Sky pale blue (white plus turquoise)

Sun rays mid yellow

Sun orange

Island and palm trees brown

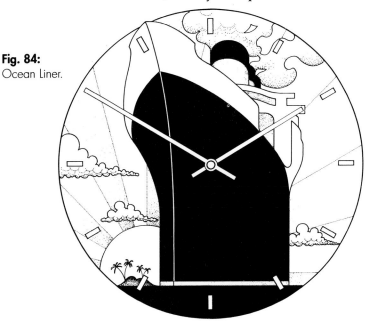

Fig. 84:
Ocean Liner.

Clouds, smoke and recess in superstructure grey (white plus black)

Funnel tops and hull black

Superstructure white

Funnels and waterline bright red

Ocean blue (ultramarine plus turquoise)

Optional Shading

Tops of clouds white

Undersides of clouds orange

Fig. 85:
Full-size pattern for Ocean Liner.

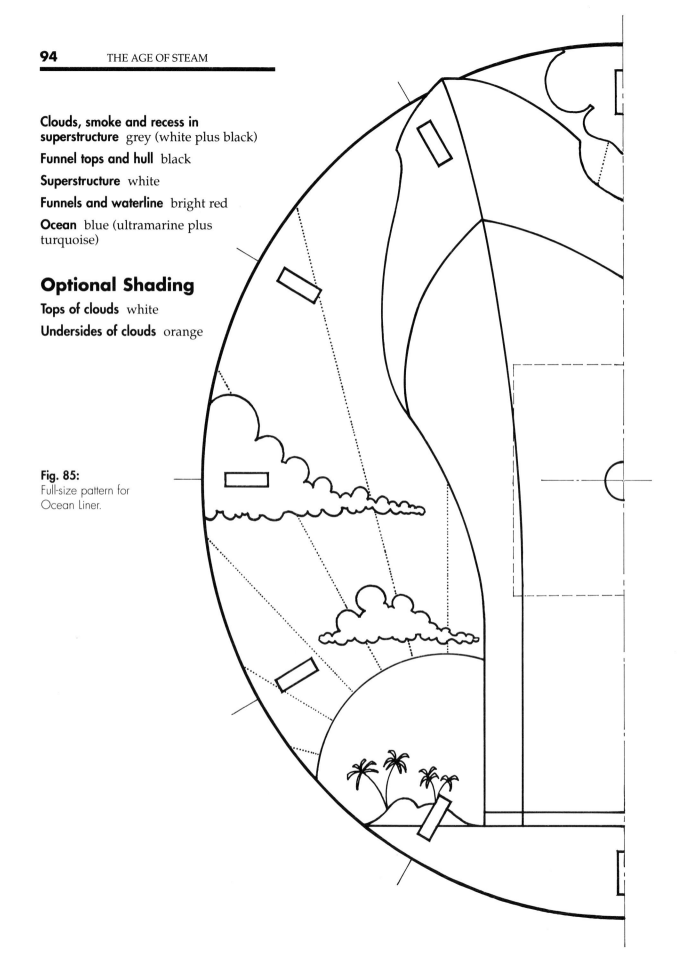

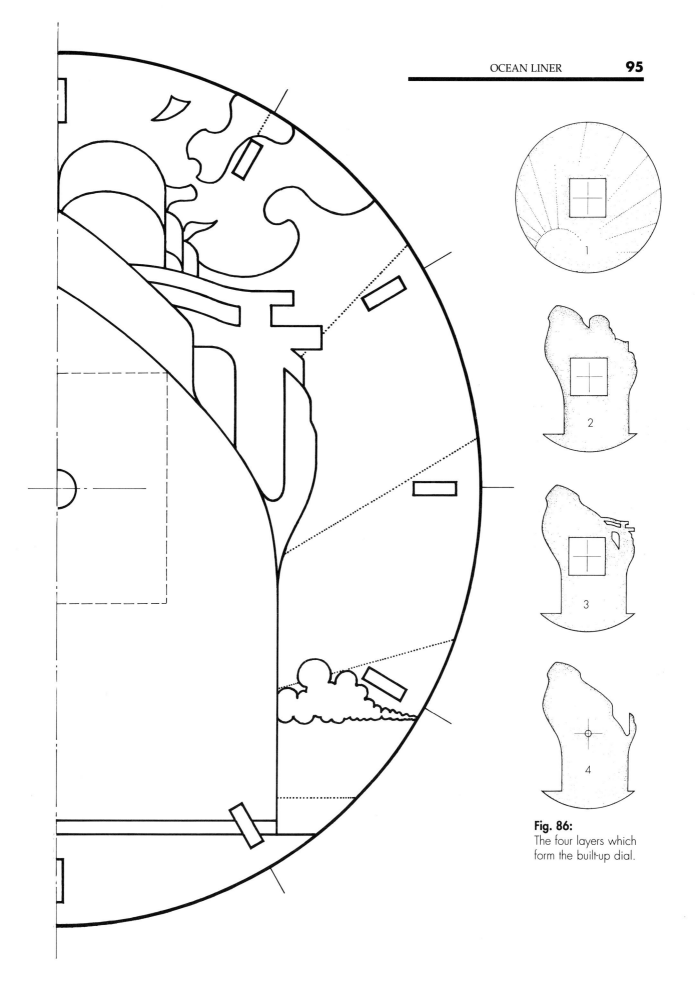

Fig. 86:
The four layers which form the built-up dial.

Materials and Parts

Smoke, clouds and island ¹⁄₁₆ in (1.5 mm) or ¹⁄₃₂ in (0.8 mm) thick plywood, 6 × 4 in (150 × 100 mm)

All other sheet parts hardboard, 18 × 18 in (460 × 460 mm)

Short spindle quartz movement with open hand fixing nut (see text)

Hands 4⅜ in (110 mm), brass

Second hand 2¾ in (70 mm), red

Hour markers ½ in (13 mm), gold finish, self-adhesive plastic

Balsa cement; paints and varnish

Ocean Liner

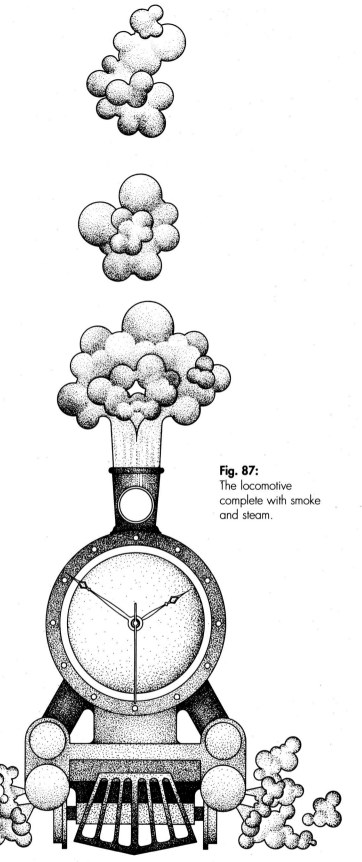

Fig. 87:
The locomotive complete with smoke and steam.

CHATTANOOGA-CHOO-CHOO

Perhaps Glenn Miller had a locomotive like this in mind when he wrote his popular song. Illustrated in both the colour photograph (page 101) and Fig. 87, the smoke, sparks and steam are optional. Showers of sparks would have been taboo in Pennsylvania station, but they contrast well with the blue of the locomotive and give the design a great feeling of unleashed energy.

Construction

The various parts which make up the locomotive are displayed in Fig. 91 (page 100) and a full-size pattern is given in Fig. 89 (page 99). The boiler parts are cut as rings in order to form a chamber for the short spindle quartz movement. If a medium spindle movement is to be fitted, leave the fourth and fifth layers (the boiler end pieces) as complete discs.

Use abrasive paper to shape the boiler end into a dome, working from coarse to fine. The top edge of the raking cow-catcher is splayed to form a good seating, and a plywood strut strengthens the arrangement. Fig. 90 (page 100) gives a section through the lower half of the locomotive, and this should help to make the construction clear.

Cement the parts together after colouring, then insert black, self-tapping screws into pre-bored holes to form hour markers.

Full-size patterns for the optional smoke and steam clouds are given in Fig. 88 (page 98). The smoke clouds are

Fig. 88:
Full-size patterns for
the smoke and steam
clouds;
(a) top smoke cloud;
(b) middle cloud;
(c) bottom cloud with
sparks;
(d) and (e) escaping
steam.

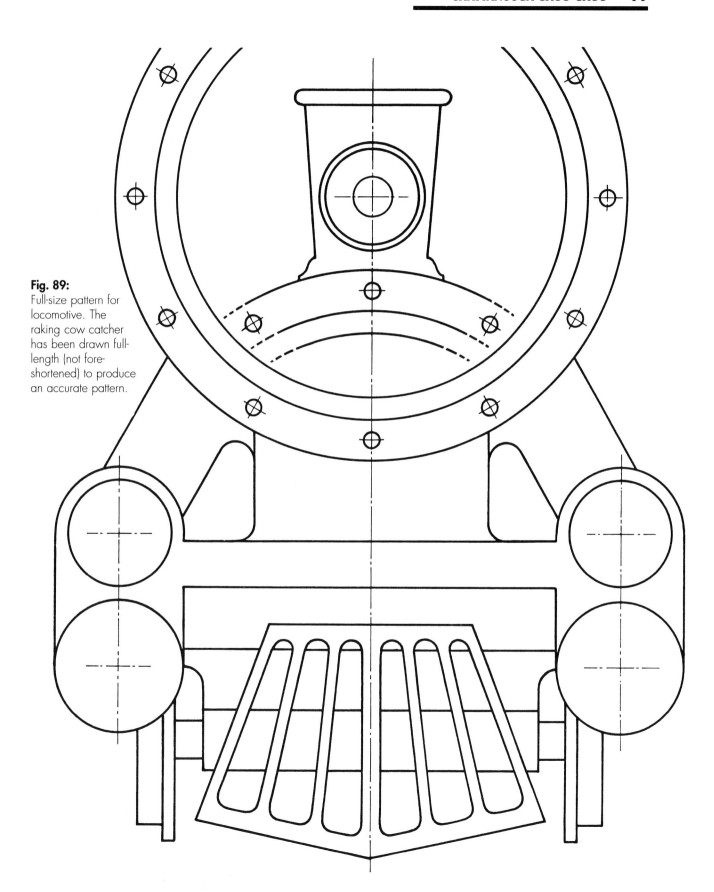

Fig. 89:
Full-size pattern for locomotive. The raking cow catcher has been drawn full-length (not fore-shortened) to produce an accurate pattern.

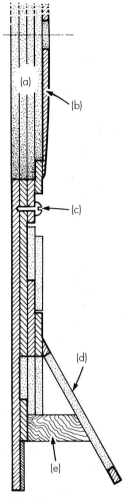

Fig. 90:
Section through lower half of locomotive (movement and hands omitted);
(a) movement chamber;
(b) boiler end;
(c) hour-marker screws;
(d) raking cow catcher;
(e) strut.

built up in two layers. Two lengths of ¹⁄₁₆ in (1.5 mm) brass wire, spaced ½ in (13 mm) apart, hold the upper clouds in position and connect them to the bottom cloud, which is cemented to the back of the locomotive. Escaping steam is modelled in three layers with isolated clouds held in place by short lengths of ¹⁄₃₂ in (0.8 mm) brass wire.

Colour Scheme

Locomotive five shades of blue ranging from pure ultramarine on the first layer to the palest blue on the boiler end. Add increasing amounts of white to produce the progressively paler shades

Lamp bright red

Sparks orange

Smoke grey (white plus black)

Steam white

Optional Shading

Chimney and cow-catcher shades of lighter and deeper blue (mix as above)

Sparks bright red and yellow

Top of smoke clouds white

Underside of clouds orange

Steam pale blue (mix as above)

Materials and Parts

Wheel flanges, chimney rim and cow-catcher strut ¹⁄₁₆ in (1.5 mm) thick plywood, 2 × 2 in (50 × 50 mm)

Locomotive, smoke and steam hardboard, 24 × 18 in (610 × 460 mm)

Short spindle quartz movement with open hand-fixing nut (a medium spindle movement can be fitted if two of the boiler layers are left intact to create sufficient panel thickness)

Hands 2½ in (65 mm), black

Second hand 2¾ in (70 mm), red

Balsa cement; twelve black, self-tapping screws, ¹⁄₁₆ × ¼ in (1.5 × 6 mm); two 12 in (305 mm) lengths of ¹⁄₁₆ in (1.5 mm) brass wire; 3 in (75 mm) length of ¹⁄₃₂ in (0.8 mm) brass wire; cotton thread; paints and varnish (wire and cotton thread are only required if the smoke and steam are provided)

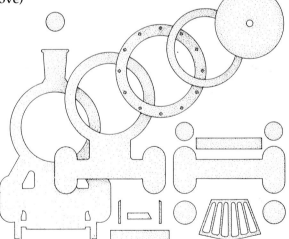

Fig. 91:
The hardboard and plywood parts which make up the clock.

Chattanooga-Choo-Choo

11 DRAGONS AND DINOSAURS

Mythical dragons and extinct dinosaurs continue to excite the imagination of the young, and some colourful examples of these fearful beasts feature on the dials of the two clocks described in this chapter.

Fig. 92:
Dragon.

DRAGON

There are clear oriental influences on the design illustrated in both the colour photograph (page 104) and Fig. 92, but the tail and bat-like wings are very much part of the Gothic tradition. A full-size pattern for the head and body is given in Fig. 93, and the legs and tail are reproduced full-size in Fig. 94 (page 105).

Construction

The head is built up in four layers, thin plywood being used for the laminate which forms the teeth. The eyelid mount extends to form the inner-ear areas and the purple mane. Each wing comprises two pieces, fanning out from the purple wing-root area which passes behind the body. All of the sheet parts which make up the clock are shown fragmented in Fig. 97 (page 106), and this should help to clarify the construction and identify the outlines of individual parts on the full-size patterns.

A rear view of the dial is given in Fig. 96 (page 106). The movement and pendulum attachment have been omitted, and the backing disc and leg and tail piece have been cut away, in order to give a clear view of the assembled sheet parts. Construction of the pendulum attachment is described and illustrated in Chapter 2. Gusseted top and bottom platforms are required with this design.

A groove must be cut in the upper wall stand-off block in order to keep it completely hidden behind the head. A simple wire hanger is secured by two screws driven into the block.

Fragmenting the design into small parts simplifies the colouring process. Dial markers were applied with the No. 2 brush, but plastic markers could be substituted if desired. Stipple the green on with a piece of sponge if difficulty is experienced obtaining an even finish.

Colour Scheme

Head, body, outer wing layers, legs and tail light green (mid green plus yellow)

Inner ear areas pale green (white plus body colour)

Nose and lower jaw dark green (mid green plus ultramarine)

Nostrils, mouth, claws, eye pupils and backing disc bright red

Wing-root area, eyelids and mane purple

Teeth white

Eye panel and clock hands mid yellow

Dial markers pale yellow (white plus mid yellow)

Optional Shading

All light green body parts dark green (mix as above) and mid yellow

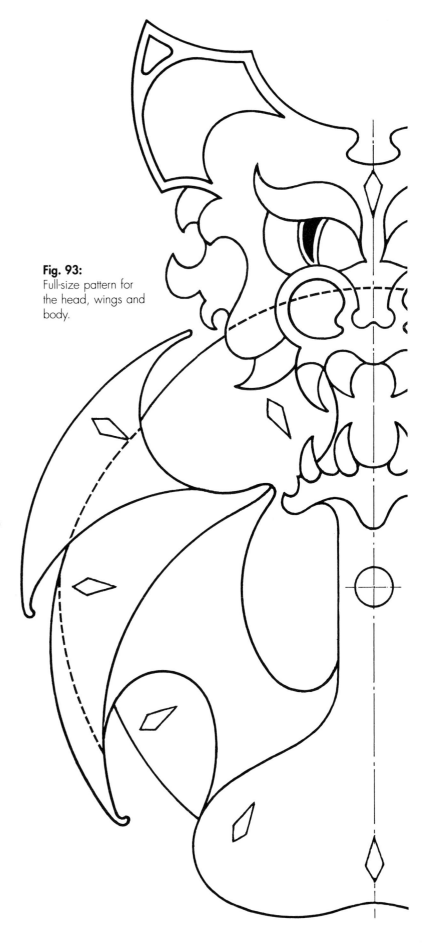

Fig. 93:
Full-size pattern for the head, wings and body.

Dragon

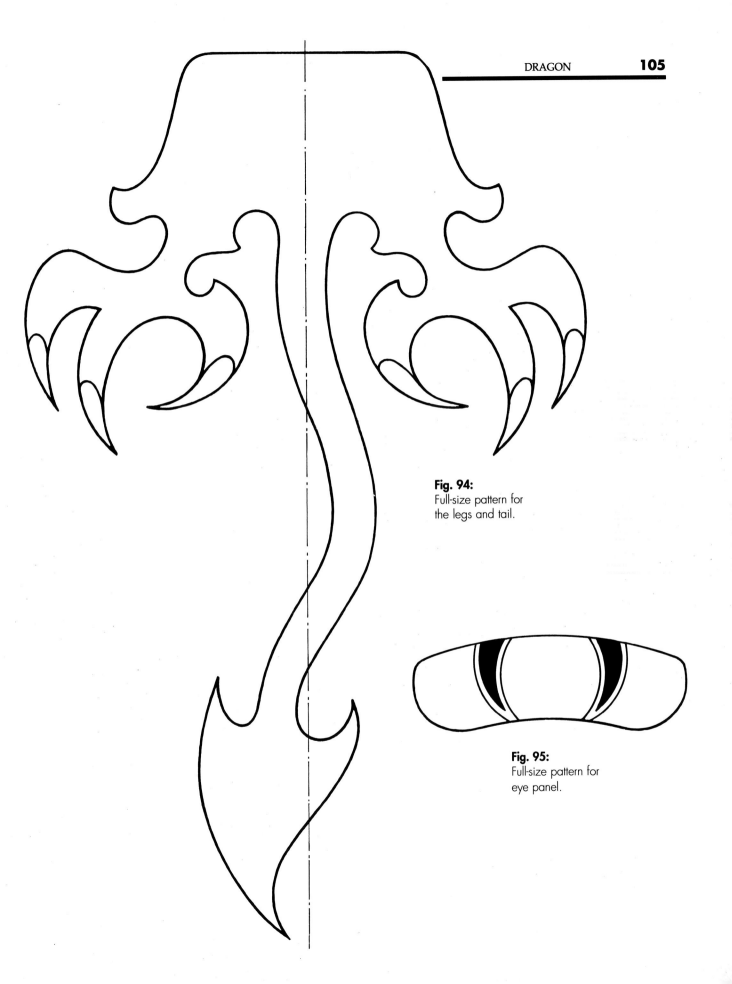

Fig. 94:
Full-size pattern for
the legs and tail.

Fig. 95:
Full-size pattern for
eye panel.

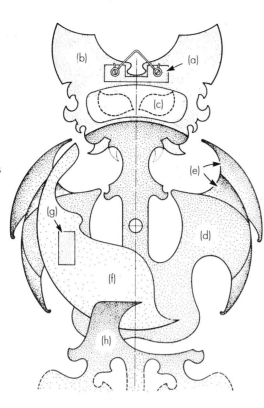

Fig. 96:
Rear view of clock with movement and pendulum attachment strip omitted and backing disc and legs cut away to reveal construction;
(a) wall stand-off block and hanger;
(b) plywood eyelid mount, inner ear areas and mane;
(c) eye panel;
(d) wing root and body back piece;
(e) wing pieces;
(f) backing disc;
(g) wall stand-off block;
(h) leg and tail piece.

Fig. 97:
The hardboard and plywood parts which make up the clock.

Backing disc where it adjoins mouth orange (to provide colour contrast with red mouth)

Upper and lower jaw pale green (mix as above)

Clock hands bright red and orange

Materials and Parts

Eyelid mount, inner ear and mane piece; pendulum attachment strip, packs, platforms and gussets; eye panel $\frac{1}{16}$ in (1.5 mm) thick plywood, 6×6 in (150×150 mm)

Teeth and claws $\frac{1}{32}$ in (0.8 mm) or $\frac{1}{64}$ in (0.4 mm), thick plywood, 3×3 in (75×75 mm)

Backing disc, head, upper and lower jaws, body, wing parts, legs and tail hardboard, 18×12 in (460×305 mm)

Wall stand-off blocks three out of a 6 in (150 mm) length of softwood, $1\frac{1}{2} \times \frac{3}{4}$ in (38×19 mm)

Long spindle quartz movement with blind hand-fixing nut

Hands $3\frac{1}{8}$ in (80 mm), brass for colouring

Balsa cement; two $\frac{3}{8}$ in (10 mm) No. 6 dome-headed brass screws and two washers; 3 in (75 mm) of $\frac{1}{32}$ in (0.8 mm) brass wire; small self-tapping screw for eye panel bracket (not required if bracket cemented in position); two small bolts for pendulum attachment, $\frac{1}{16}$ in (1.5 mm) maximum diameter $\times \frac{3}{8}$ in (10 mm) long, complete with nuts; self-adhesive paper label (for eyes); paints and varnish

VALLEY OF THE DINOSAURS

Pterodactyls fly over a hot, primordial landscape where dinosaurs roam. The clock is illustrated in both the colour photograph (page 109) and Fig. 98.

Construction

Difficult brushwork is reduced as far as possible by building up the dial in five layers. The second and third layers are cut from ¹⁄₁₆ in (1.5 mm) plywood in order to limit the thickness of the complete assembly. Despite this, a long spindle quartz movement will not ensure sufficient hand clearance above the numerals, and the hands must be bent, as illustrated in Fig. 10 on page 24.

The pterodactyls and three of the dinosaurs (tyrannosaurus, stegosaurus and iguanodon) are cut from ¹⁄₁₆ in (1.5 mm) plywood and cemented to the dial after colouring. The brontosaurus striding out of the three o'clock position forms part of the hardboard fourth layer.

Distant volcanoes are painted on to the first layer with the No. 2 brush, and compasses with a ruling pen attachment can be used to form a clean, circular outline for the sun. Alternatively, these items can be cut from thin plywood and stuck down after colouring.

The five layers of the dial are shown separately in Fig. 100 (page 110). This should help when identifying part outlines in the full-size pattern given in Fig. 101 (page 110). Plywood dinosaurs are omitted from the pattern in the

interests of clarity. They are reproduced full-size in Fig. 99 (page 108).

Washers or a spacing sleeve must be placed beneath the movement fixing screw. This is described and illustrated in Chapter 2.

The optional pendulum is shown in Fig. 102. The hardboard is cut into very slender sections at some points on its circumference. If there is any fraying, rub balsa cement into the edge of the board and squeeze the fibres together.

Fig. 98:
The Valley of the Dinosaurs.

Colour Scheme

Sky yellow (mid yellow plus white)

Pterodactyls deep purple (purple plus a hint of black)

Sun bright red

Distant mountains and second, third and fourth layers of dial various shades of mauve (red plus blue plus increasing amounts of white as the hills recede. The distant mountains on the first layer are almost all white with just a hint of the red and blue)

Fifth layer (foreground) deep red (bright red plus a hint of ultramarine)

Dinosaurs various shades of green (add ultramarine to mid green or mid green to yellow to produce the different colours)

Pendulum rod yellow (same mix as sky)

Pendulum purple

Optional Shading

Sun orange

Mauve hills deeper shades of mauve (mix as above)

Dinosaurs deeper or lighter shades of green (mix as above)

Fifth layer (foreground) bright red

Pendulum bob deep red (mix as above)

Materials and Parts

First, fourth and fifth layers of the dial and the pendulum rod and bob hardboard, 21 × 15 in (535 × 380 mm)

Pterodactyls, three of the dinosaurs and layers two and three of the dial 1/16 in (1.5 mm) thick plywood, 15 × 9 in (380 × 230 mm)

Long spindle quartz movement with blind hand-fixing nut

Hands 4⅜ in (110 mm), brass

Numerals ⅞ in (22 mm) gold finish, self-adhesive plastic

Balsa cement; 3 in (75 mm) length of 1/32 in (0.8 mm) brass wire; cotton thread; washers or card sleeve for movement fixing screw; paints and varnish

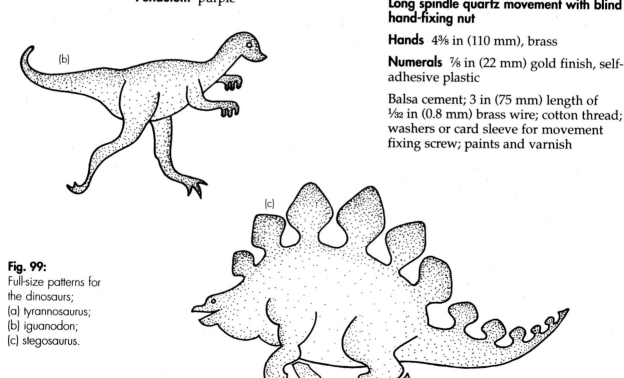

Fig. 99:
Full-size patterns for the dinosaurs;
(a) tyrannosaurus;
(b) iguanodon;
(c) stegosaurus.

Valley of the Dinosaurs

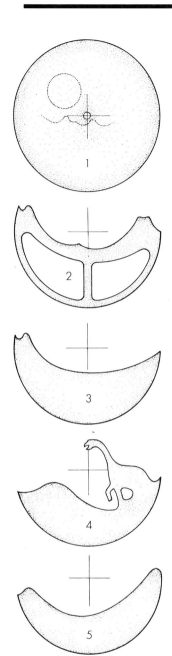

Fig. 100:
The five layers which form the built-up dial. Second and third layers are plywood; the rest hardboard. Hidden areas of plywood can be cut away and used for the pterodactyls.

Fig. 101:
Full-size pattern for the Valley of the Dinosaurs.

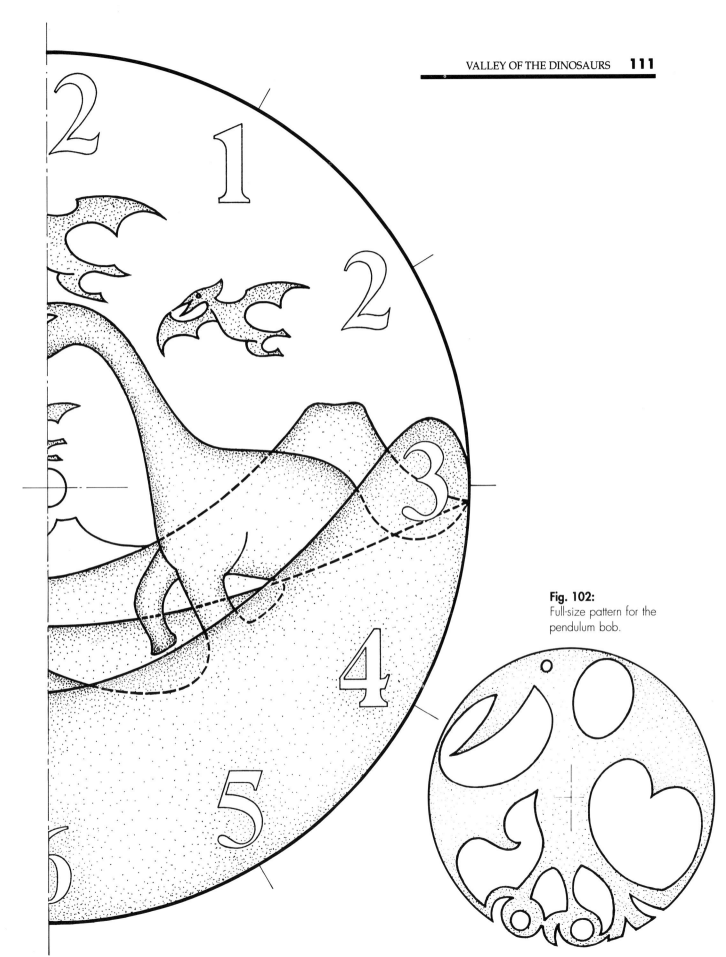

Fig. 102:
Full-size pattern for the pendulum bob.

12 TWO SURREAL TIMEPIECES

The bizarre, dream-like quality of the surreal is evident in these two clock designs.

SALVADOR'S WATCH

Inspired by the melting watches in Salvador Dali's painting 'The Disintegration of the Persistence of Memory', this timepiece is illustrated in both the colour photograph and Fig. 105 (page 114).

A surreal landscape with receding perspectives and obscure images fills the dial of a watch which is about to melt away. The hinge, catch and winder add to the dreamlike reality of the creation, and one of the droplets of molten metal forms the swinging pendulum.

Construction

This clock is formed in only two layers: the dial piece, which carries the picture, and the frame which is stuck down on top of the dial after both parts have been coloured. The dial piece and frame are cut to the same, curving outline. The hinge and catch are cut separately and cemented in position. The winder is built up in three layers, and full-size patterns for all of the parts are given in Fig. 103 (opposite).

The pendulum bob is suspended from the plastic arm on the quartz movement

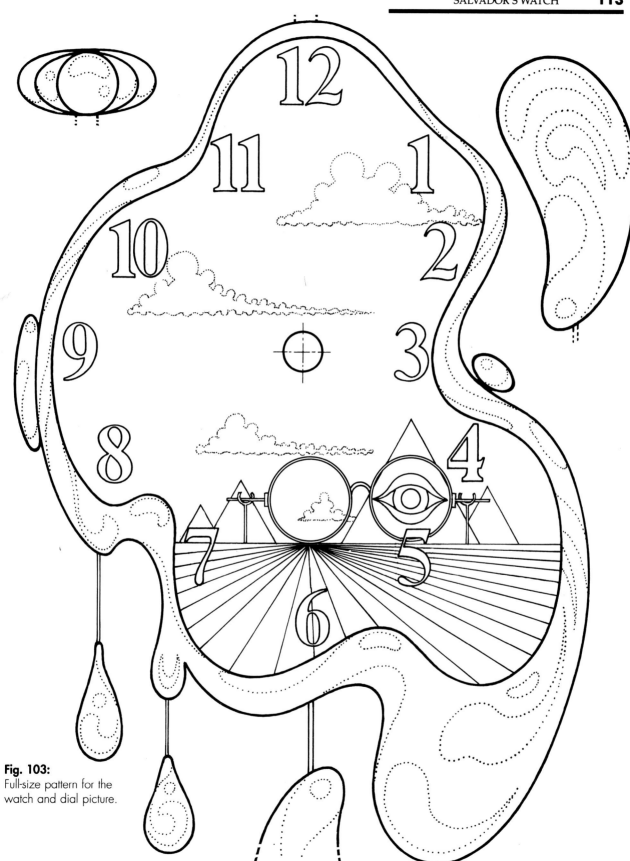

Fig. 103:
Full-size pattern for the
watch and dial picture.

Fig. 104:
Hook for pendulum rod.

Fig. 105:
Salvador's Watch.

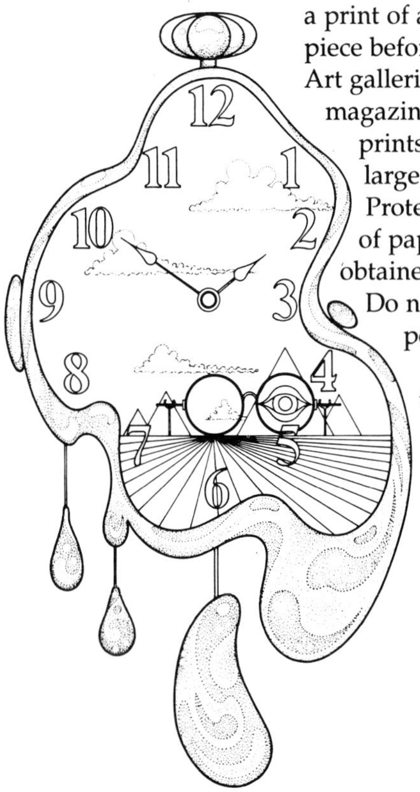

by a length of 1/16 in (1.5 mm) diameter brass wire. Fig. 104 (left) shows how the wire is bent to hook over the cradle on the plastic arm. The other two hardboard droplets are hung from the dial by short lengths of 1/32 in (0.8 mm) diameter brass wire. Bind the ends of the wires with cotton thread and rub in a liberal application of balsa cement so that they can be attached to the hardboard parts, all as described in Chapter 2.

The colouring which simulates the gold of a watch case is easy to duplicate, and the outlines of shadows and highlights are reproduced on the full-size pattern. If preferred, these outlines can be transferred to the frame and droplets after the background colour has been applied.

Painting the landscape on the dial does call for care and patience, however, and a ruling pen and compasses with a pen attachment will make the task much easier. This effort can be avoided, and a more authentic effect created, by pasting a print of a Dali painting on to the dial piece before the frame is stuck down. Art galleries, picture framers and art magazines are good sources of suitable prints. If the reproduction is too large, paste down a selected area. Protect the surface with two coats of paper varnish which can be obtained from artists' supply shops. Do not use the oil-based polyurethane varnish as this will make the paper translucent and ruin the effect.

Colour Scheme

Watch Case:

Background colour mid yellow

Light areas pale yellow (white plus mid yellow)

Highlights white

Shadows orange

Picture on the Dial:

Sky blue (white plus ultramarine plus turquoise)

Clouds white

Pyramids pinkish buff (white plus brown plus red)

Eyelids flesh pink (white plus red plus brown)

Eye white, pale blue (white plus sky colour) and blue (sky colour)

Foreground and spectacle supports reddish brown (red plus brown)

Spectacles and perspective lines on foreground bright red

Hands and numerals pale yellow (mix as above), mid yellow and orange

Materials and Parts

All the watch parts hardboard, 15 × 12 in (380 × 305 mm)

Short spindle quartz movement with blind hand-fixing nut (a medium spindle unit can be used if a hardboard washer is placed beneath the dial)

Hands 1 5/8 in (41 mm), brass for colouring

Numerals 5/8 in (16 mm), self-adhesive plastic

Balsa cement; 6 in (150 mm) of 1/16 in (1.5 mm) brass wire; 6 in (150 mm) of 1/32 in (0.8 mm) brass wire; cotton thread; paints and varnish. (Refer to text for details of optional Dali print and paper varnish)

THE SWINGING SAUSAGE

This clock is shown in both the colour photograph (page 117) and Fig. 106. Egg, bacon, beans and chips are frozen in their downward slide, but a few beans have managed to drop free and hitch a ride on the swinging sausage.

Construction

A full-size pattern for the plate, sausage and fork is given in Fig. 108 (page 116). Egg and bacon rashers are reproduced full-size in Fig. 110 (page 118).

The plate is built up from a disc and a ring of hardboard. The knife and fork consist of a plywood blade or tines sandwiched between the two pieces of hardboard which form the handle, and a small piece of plywood represents the ferrule, all as illustrated in Fig. 107.

Two thicknesses of hardboard are used for the sausage pendulum bob, and small pieces of plywood, inserted into the ends, simulate the knots in the skin.

The knife, fork and plate are mounted on the table-cloth backing panel. The panel is cut away beneath the plate, and the four self-tapping screws which secure the plate are passed through hardboard spacers to lift it clear of the panel. These measures provide clearance for the brass strip which connects the sausage pendulum bob to the quartz movement. The section given in Fig. 109 (page 118) should help to clarify the construction. Make sure that the screws are not too long or they will pierce the rim of the plate. There is not a lot of clearance for the moving parts, and the

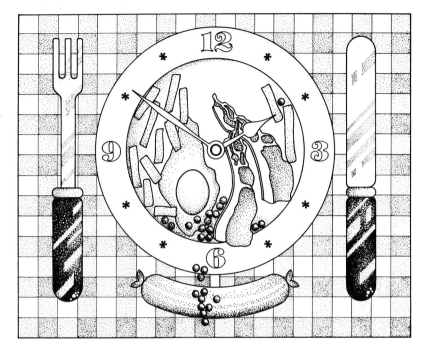

Fig. 106:
The Swinging
Sausage.

sausage is best attached to the brass strip with a square of masking tape.

The rashers of bacon and the white of the egg are cut from 1⁄64 in (0.4 mm) plywood. Egg yolk and chips are cut from hardboard. The beans are 1⁄4 in (6 mm) diameter plastic beads, primed with emulsion paint before colouring. Cut the chips with wavy outlines, about 1⁄4 in (6 mm) wide and ranging from 1⁄2 in (13 mm) to 11⁄2 in (38 mm) long. One of the bacon rashers is carried over the rim of the plate and the thin plywood is desirable for its flexibility and for maintaining hand clearance.

The numerals were drawn on to the plate with a No. 2 brush, but 3⁄8 in (10 mm) or 1⁄2 in (13 mm) rub-down transfers would be suitable.

Fig. 107:
Sandwich construction
of knife and fork;
(a) hardboard handle
parts;
(b) plywood blade;
(c) plywood ferrule.

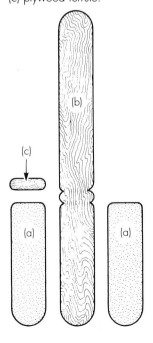

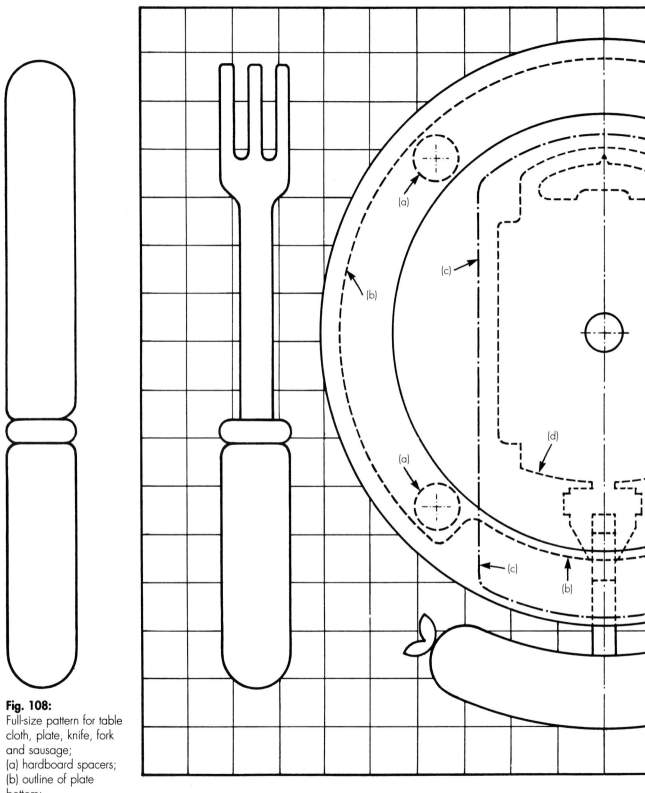

Fig. 108:
Full-size pattern for table
cloth, plate, knife, fork
and sausage;
(a) hardboard spacers;
(b) outline of plate
bottom;
(c) outline of hole in
table cloth;
(d) movement.

Colour Scheme

Table cloth pale yellow (white plus mid yellow)

Plate white (emulsion paint)

Chips yellow (mid yellow plus white)

Egg yolk mid yellow

Beans deep orange (orange plus red)

Bacon deep red (bright red plus brown plus white)

Bacon fat off white (white plus yellow plus brown)

Bacon rind light brown (white plus brown)

Sausage light brown (white plus brown plus red)

Knife and fork handles blue (turquoise plus ultramarine)

Knife and fork metal parts pale blue (white plus turquoise plus a hint of black)

Hands blue (mix as above)

Second hand deep orange (mix as above)

The Swinging Sausage

Optional Shading and Decorations

Plate blue lines drawn around rim with compasses fitted with a ruling pen attachment (blue mixed as above)

Chips pale orange (white plus orange)

Egg white pale brown (white plus brown)

Beans tint some beans a deeper and some a lighter shade of orange

Bacon bright red

Sausage paler brown (white plus brown), brown

Knife and fork metal parts white

Numerals blue (mix as above but see text and parts list)

Materials and Parts

Knife blade, fork tines and ferrules ¹⁄₁₆ in (1.5 mm) thick plywood, 7 × 2 in (180 × 50 mm)

Bacon, egg white and sausage ties ¹⁄₆₄ in (0.8 mm) thick plywood, 4 × 4 in (100 × 100 mm)

All other sheet parts, including egg yolk, chips, two-layer sausage, and knife and fork handles hardboard, 15 × 12 in (380 × 305 mm)

Medium spindle quartz movement with open hand-fixing nut

Hands 2½ in (65 mm), brass, for colouring

Seconds hand 2¾ in (70 mm), red or brass, for colouring

Numerals ⅜ in (10 mm) or ½ in (13 mm) rub-down transfer

Balsa cement; four ⅜ × ¹⁄₁₆ in (10 × 1.5 mm) self-tapping screws; 3 in (75 mm) of brass strip, ¼ × ¹⁄₃₂ in (6 × 0.8 mm); paints and varnish

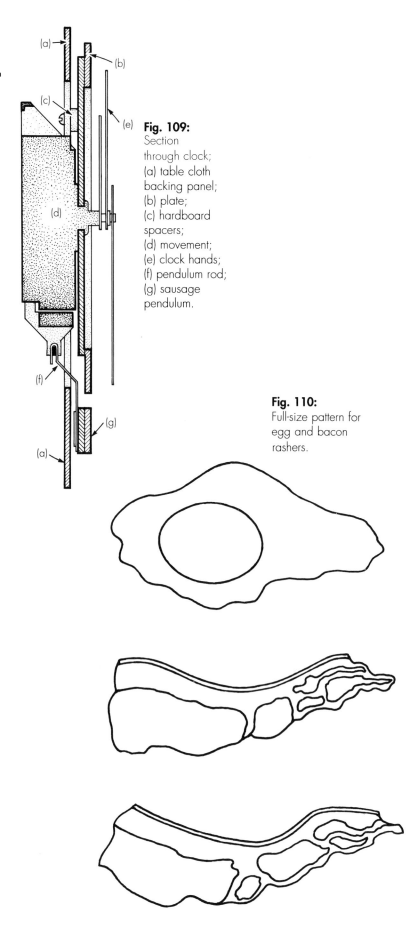

Fig. 109:
Section through clock;
(a) table cloth backing panel;
(b) plate;
(c) hardboard spacers;
(d) movement;
(e) clock hands;
(f) pendulum rod;
(g) sausage pendulum.

Fig. 110:
Full-size pattern for egg and bacon rashers.

13 CELESTIAL CLOCKS

Sun, moons and stars decorate the dials and pendulums of these two contrasting timepieces.

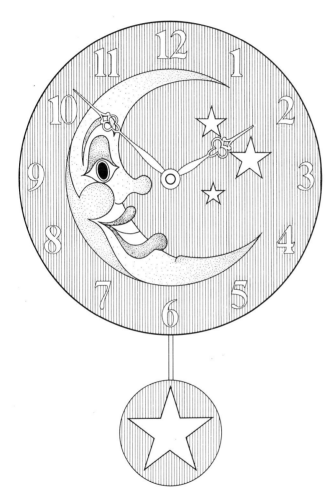

Fig. 111:
Mr Moon.

MR MOON

The Man in the Moon has a wicked grin and starlight seems to be twinkling in his eye. Illustrated in both the colour photograph (page 121) and Fig. 111, this jolly concoction will brighten the walls of any nursery.

Construction

The moon and scattering of stars are reproduced full-size in Fig. 112, and the optional pendulum in Fig. 114 (page 120). Moon, stars and plastic numerals are stuck down on a 9⅛ in (233 mm) diameter backing disc after colouring.

The eyelid is formed from plastic wood built up on a plywood mount which also carries the eye parts. Shave away a thin layer of hardboard on the underside of the moon, just big enough to house the eyelid mount, so that the moon can bed evenly on the backing disc. The hardboard cheek piece and the plywood lips and eyebrow are cemented in position after colouring, all as shown in Fig. 113 (page 120).

Colour Scheme

Backing disc and pendulum bob blue (ultramarine and turquoise)

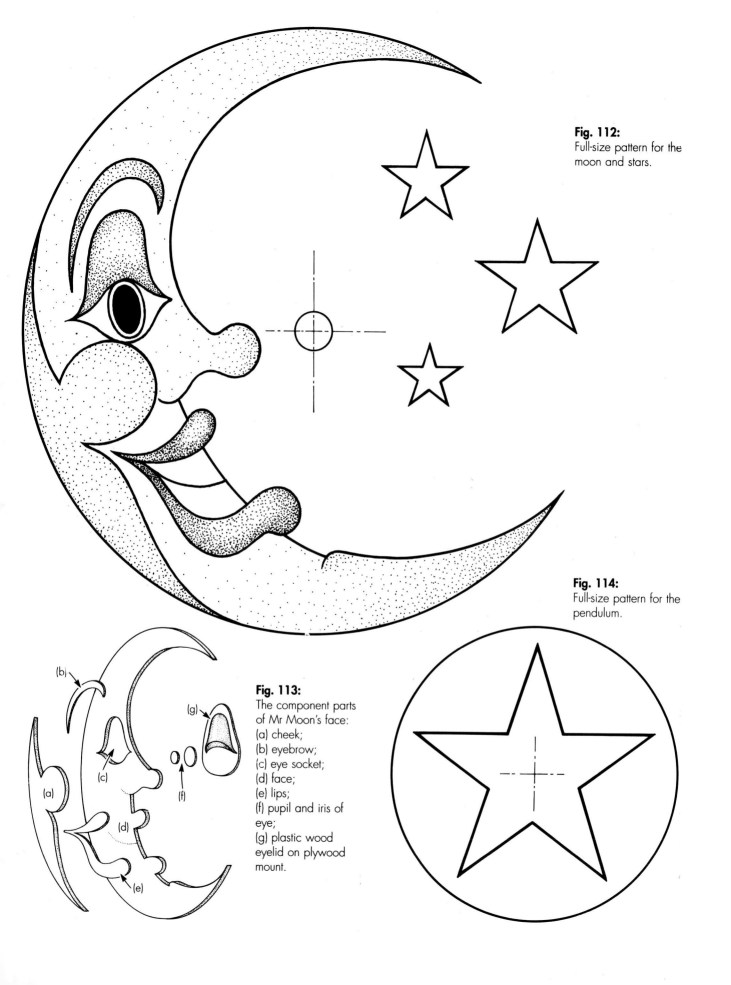

Fig. 112:
Full-size pattern for the moon and stars.

Fig. 114:
Full-size pattern for the pendulum.

Fig. 113:
The component parts of Mr Moon's face:
(a) cheek;
(b) eyebrow;
(c) eye socket;
(d) face;
(e) lips;
(f) pupil and iris of eye;
(g) plastic wood eyelid on plywood mount.

Moon face, stars, pendulum rod, hands and numerals pale yellow (white plus mid yellow)

Lips red (bright red plus a hint of brown)

Teeth and eye panel white

Eye iris pale blue (white plus turquoise)

Eye pupil blue (turquoise)

Optional Shading

Moon face, cheeks, eyelid, eyebrow, hands, numerals, stars and pendulum rod mid yellow, orange

Materials and Parts

Backing disc, pendulum bob, pendulum rod, two large stars, moon and moon cheek hardboard, 15 × 12 in (380 × 305 mm)

Eyebrow, eye iris and pupil, lips and two small stars ¹⁄₁₆ in (1.5 mm) thick plywood, 4 × 2 in (100 × 50 mm)

Eyelid plastic wood

Eyelid mount ¹⁄₃₂ in (0.8 mm) or ¹⁄₆₄ in (0.4 mm) thick plywood, 2 × 1½ in (50 × 38 mm)

Medium spindle quartz movement with blind hand-fixing nut (the hands will need bending slightly to clear the eyelid, as illustrated in Fig. 10, page 24)

Hands 3⅞ in (98 mm), brass for colouring

Numerals ⅞ in (22 mm), self-adhesive plastic

Balsa cement; 3 in (75 mm) of ¹⁄₃₂ in (0.8 mm) brass wire; cotton thread; paints and varnish

Mr Moon

Fig. 115:
The Sun, Moon and
Stars.

Fig. 116:
Full-size pattern for the
sun's face.

SUN, MOON AND STARS

This clock, the largest timepiece in the collection, is illustrated in both the colour photograph (page 125) and Fig. 115. A constellation of stars drifts above the sun while the moon swings serenely below.

Construction

Full-size patterns for the dial, solar flares, pendulum and stars are given in Figs. 116 (page 122), 117, 119 (page 126) and 120 (page 126). The hardboard and plywood parts which make up the dial are shown in Fig. 121 (page 127), and the

pendulum in Fig. 122 (page 127). They are assembled after colouring.

The two sets of solar flares, one straight-sided and one wavy, are separated by a ½ in (13 mm) wide ring of hardboard. Draw a 6⅞ in (175 mm) diameter circle on scrap paper and assemble the two sets of flares with their separating ring on this. Use a straight edge to check that opposite points around the dial are in line. Cement the parts together when the setting out is satisfactory.

Constructors who wish to apply stencilled numerals should do so now, before the flare assembly is cemented to the dial. Full details of the technique, including the preliminary varnishing, are given in Chapter 2. The 1 in (25 mm) numerals stencilled on to the Duck and Ducklings clock (page 32) were used for this timepiece also.

The eyelids for the sun and moon are formed from plastic wood built up on plywood mounts which also carry the eye parts.

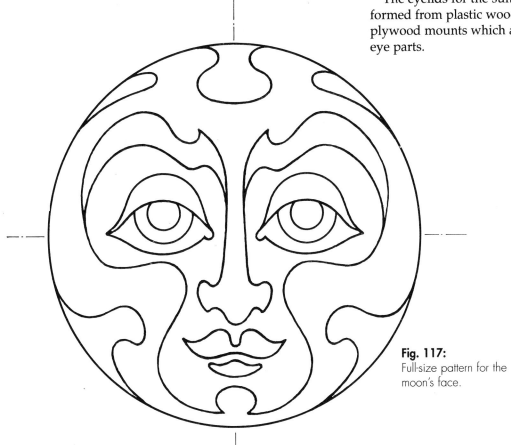

Fig. 117:
Full-size pattern for the moon's face.

The rear view of the clock, Fig. 118 (below), shows the wires which connect the stars to the plywood pendulum extension. A wire hook on the moon pendulum rod attaches it to the cradle on the quartz movement in the usual way. Locate a cross wire, just hidden behind the rim of the dial, and bind and cement it to the wires which connect the stars. This will make the constellation more rigid.

Cut a 'V'-shaped notch in the strip of plywood linking the upper stand-off blocks to provide a means of hanging the clock.

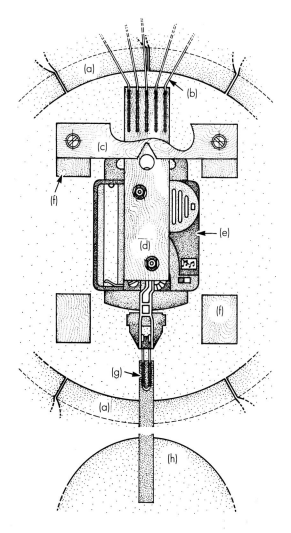

Colour Scheme for the Sun

Flares orange and mid yellow

First layer of face, eyebrows, cheek and chin decoration mid yellow

Second layer of face pale yellow (white plus mid yellow)

Forehead decoration yellow (mid yellow plus white)

Area within forehead decoration, tip of nose and eye panels very pale yellow (white plus mid yellow)

Eyelids pale orange (orange plus white)

Lips and eye irises orange

Eye pupils and numerals bright red

Hands orange (optional shading: red and mid yellow)

Colour Scheme for the Moon and Stars

Moon five shades of blue, ranging from pure ultramarine on the eye pupils to a very pale blue on the first layer at the perimeter of the bob (make the shades of blue by adding various amounts of ultramarine to white)

Eye panels and stars white

Pendulum rod blue (ultramarine)

Fig. 118:
Rear view of dial with wall-hanger strip cut away to reveal wires connecting the stars;
(a) solar flares;
(b) wires;
(c) wall-hanger strip;
(d) pendulum attachment strip;
(e) movement;
(f) wall stand-off blocks;
(g) pendulum rod;
(h) pendulum bob.

Sun, Moon and Stars

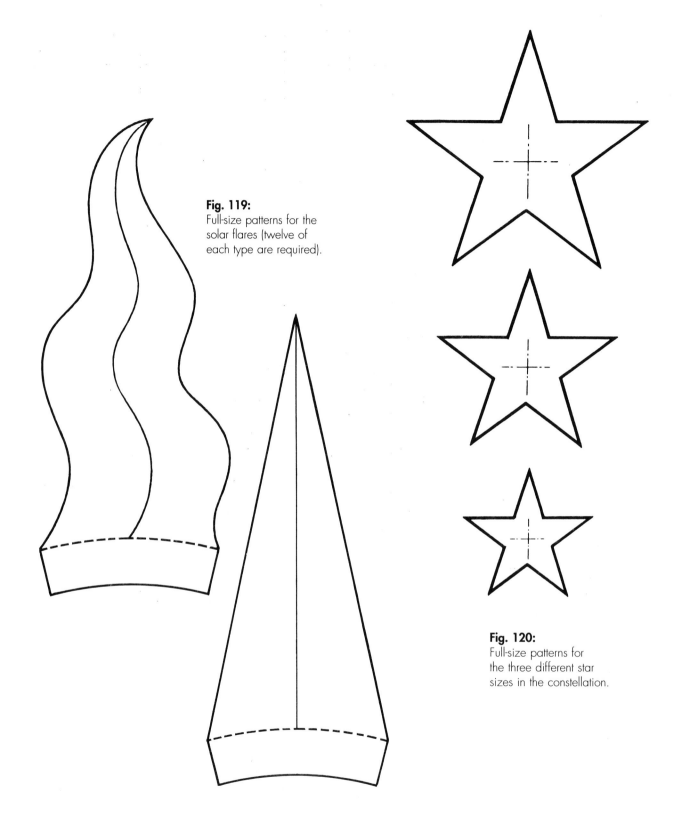

Fig. 119:
Full-size patterns for the
solar flares (twelve of
each type are required).

Fig. 120:
Full-size patterns for
the three different star
sizes in the constellation.

Materials and Parts

Pendulum attachment strip and packs; hanger strip, sun and moon eye pupils, decorations to forehead, cheeks and chin of sun ¹⁄₁₆ in (1.5 mm) thick plywood, 6 × 6 in (150 × 150 mm)

Eyelid mounts ¹⁄₃₂ in (0.8 mm) thick plywood, 5 × 3 in (125 × 75 mm)

All other sheet parts hardboard, 36 × 24 in (915 × 610 mm)

Wall stand-off blocks four out of a 6 in (150 mm) length of softwood, 1½ × 1 in (38 × 25 mm)

Stencil thin acetate or plastic sheet, 11½ × 8 in (295 × 210 mm)

Medium spindle quartz movement with blind hand-fixing nut

Hands 3⅞ in (98 mm), brass for colouring

Balsa cement; 3 in (75 mm) length of ¹⁄₃₂ in (0.8 mm) brass wire; six 12 in (305 mm) lengths of ³⁄₆₄ in (1 mm) brass wire; two ½ in (12 mm) No. 6 brass screws; two small bolts for pendulum attachment, ¹⁄₁₆ in (1.5 mm) maximum diameter × ⅜ in (10 mm) long, complete with nuts; cotton thread; paints and varnish

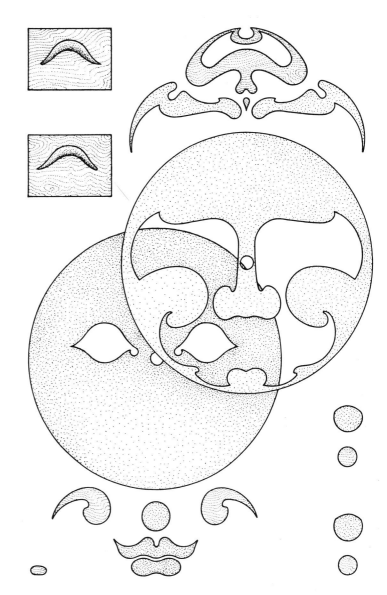

Fig. 121:
The hardboard and plywood parts which make up the sun. (The twenty-four solar flares and the separating ring for the flares are not included in the illustration.)

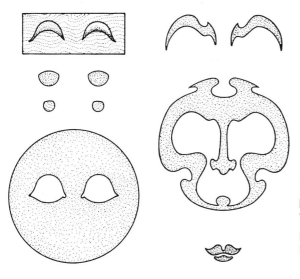

Fig. 122:
The hardboard and plywood parts which make up the moon.

INDEX